Patterns for World Cultures

Written and illustrated by
Marilynn G. Barr

TRAVEL KENYA

Publisher: Roberta Suid
Copy Editor: Carol Whiteley
Design and Production: MGB Press

Monday Morning Books is a registered trademark of
Monday Morning Books, Inc.

Entire contents copyright © 1995
by Monday Morning Books, Inc., Box 1680, Palo Alto, California 94302

For a complete catalog, write to the address above.

ISBN 1-878279-76-9

Printed in the United States of America

9 8 7 6 5 4 3 2 1

TABLE OF CONTENTS

Introduction

Take your students on a journey to a country in Africa, Asia, Australia, Europe, or South America; to a North American Hopi settlement; or to the ancient civilizations of China, Rome, Egypt, and Mexico with *Patterns for World Cultures.*

Patterns for World Cultures includes maps and patterns for a dwelling, people, foods, tools, animals, vehicles, and landmarks for ten different world cultures. Pattern pages include basic information about cultural traditions, geography, history, and natural resources.

Your students will also enjoy making their own crafts, such as Egyptian collars or Carnaval headdresses. Literature Links will introduce students to featured storybooks about these unique cultures.

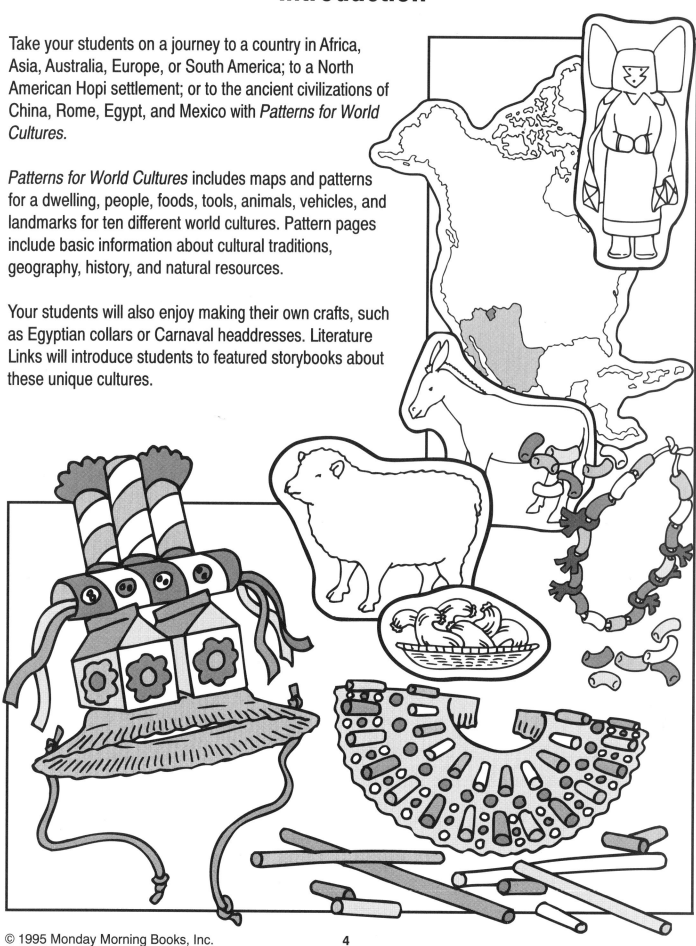

How to Use the Patterns

- The actual patterns can be used to create dioramas, collages, mobiles, and hand puppets. They can also be used as visuals for student reports.
- Patterns can be enlarged for bulletin board displays or puppet theater productions.
- Students can use the patterns as templates or as references to create their own images.

For Dioramas

Provide students with the materials listed below to create dramatic dioramas.

- corrugated board — a large sheet can be used as a platform
- spools — attach to backs to make free-standing patterns
- crepe paper — to decorate the inside or outside of the shoe box
- old silk flowers — for landscapes or decorating
- Popsicle sticks — to use as wooden beams, flooring, fencing, or roofing
- aluminum foil — for roofing, windows, or jewelry
- plastic wrap — for windows or to create the illusion of water
- bark mulch — for landscapes or painted to resemble rocks
- pine straw — for roofing or to make hay or wheat stacks
- craft tissue — to create flames
- cotton balls — to create clouds or cotton fields
- scrap cloth — for woven cloth props or to attach to patterns
- clay — to make pottery and sculptures
- brown grocery bags — to use for stucco or mud brick buildings
- large buttons — can be used as plates and serving pieces
- pipe cleaners — can be formed into tools, necklaces, and other props

For Collages

Students can use the patterns to create colorful collages showing a variety of items from one culture.

For instance, to make a cultural collage, provide students with enlarged maps of Africa and Kenya. Have students color, cut out, and glue the maps to a sheet of poster board.

Then provide students with the patterns for Kenya. Also provide magazines for additional cut-out pictures, and a variety of craft supplies for students to complete their Kenyan Cultural Collage.

For Hand Puppets

The people and animal patterns can be used to make hand puppets. Have children color and cut out the patterns.

To make hand puppets using Popsicle sticks, have children apply glue to one end of a stick and attach it to the back of a pattern.

To make hand puppets using paper bags, have children apply glue to the backs of patterns and attach each one to a separate bag.

To make hand puppets using old gloves or mittens, have children apply glue to the back of a pattern and attach it to the palm side of an old glove or mitten.

For Book Report Visuals

Show students how to create book report visuals. Provide children with construction paper, crayons, scissors, glue, and patterns for a book report on a specific world culture.

Demonstrate how to cut various size and shape frames from construction paper. Then show how to use the frames to highlight patterns, drawings, or cutouts used as visuals.

For Bulletin Board Displays

Enlarge patterns to display on your bulletin board. For a 3-D effect, attach various size box lids to the backs of patterns before mounting on the board.

Trace and cut clothing for people from wallpaper or cloth scraps. Add buttons, feathers, and other craft materials.

For a student work display board, reproduce a dwelling pattern for each student to color and cut out. Provide a sheet of construction paper, crayons, scissors, and glue.

Show students how to fold construction paper for a booklet cover. They can glue the cut-out dwelling on the front. Attach booklet covers to the board.

Trace the outline of the same dwelling pattern on white paper for students to practice writing and other class work. Have students insert completed assignments in their dwelling booklets.

For Puppet Theater Productions

Enlarge patterns to make a puppet theater using the bulletin board as the background and a large cardboard box on a table as the working theater.

Decorate your bulletin board with patterns from one of the world cultures in this book. Position a table in front of the bulletin board decorated with matching terrain. Cover and cut a window in a large cardboard box to look like a dwelling on the board. For a brick structure, cover the box with brown paper bags. Use crumpled white construction paper for stucco. Use hay, straw, or green construction paper for thatched dwellings.

Provide students with patterns to color and cut out to make puppets and props.

Then help students prepare a script and perform a play about the people of the community entitled "A Day in the Life of a ___." Invite parents to attend the performance.

As Templates

Students can use the patterns in this book as resources to create their own drawings or patterns. They can also use the actual patterns (cut out and colored) to make mobiles, greeting cards, or to paste in scrapbooks. Students can also use the patterns as templates to create outline drawings, which they can decorate themselves.

Show students how to trace around cut-out patterns. Then show how to add features and other details.

For Mobiles

Provide students with hangers, paper plates, or corrugated board to form a mobile base.

Once children have colored and cut out patterns, show how to punch a hole in each pattern. Tie yarn to patterns and attach loose ends to the mobile base. Hang finished mobiles from your classroom ceiling.

For Scrapbooks

Provide students with oak tag, colored construction paper pages, crayons, scissors, and glue to make scrapbooks.

Have each child make and decorate a scrapbook cover. Punch two holes along the left side of the cover and scrapbook pages. Insert construction paper pages between the book covers. Lace and tie a length of yarn or ribbon through the holes of the scrapbook.

For Greetings and Posters

Provide students with construction paper, poster board, crayons, scissors, glue, and patterns to make greeting cards or posters.

Map: Africa

Kenya is located in east-central Africa with the Indian
Ocean on its southeastern shores.

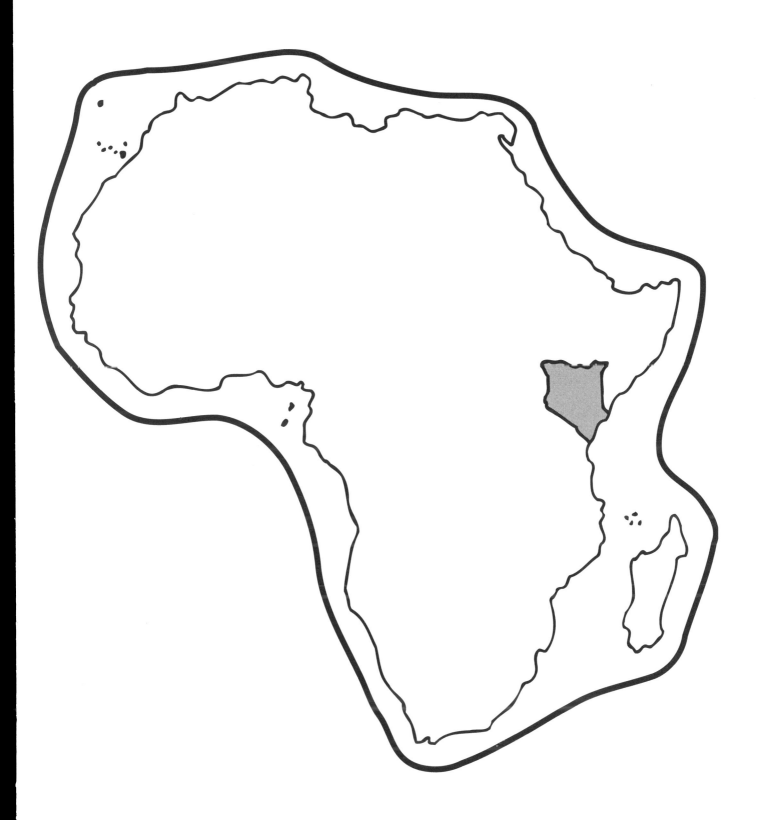

Map: Kenya

Kenya lies between the Somali Republic, the Sudan, Ethiopia, Uganda, and Tanzania.

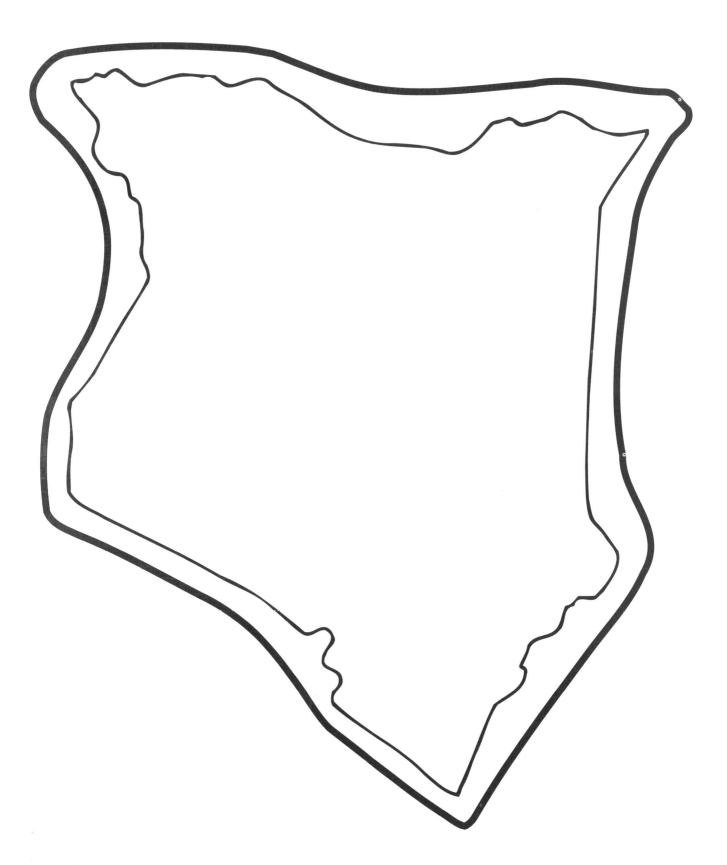

Bulletin Board: A Community in Kenya

1. Enlarge the patterns on pages 12-18.
2. Color and cut out the patterns.
3. Cover your bulletin board with pale blue paper at the top and brown at the bottom.
4. Add a green or red colored border.
5. Enlarge, color, and cut out the title below.
6. Arrange and attach the patterns to your bulletin board.

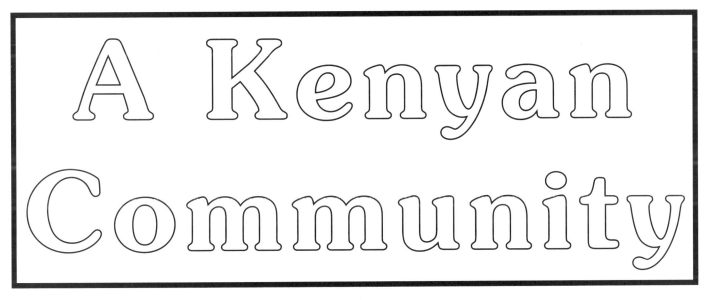

Bulletin Board Patterns: A Dwelling in Kenya

Some families in Kenya live in dwellings made from cement block walls and palm leaf roofs. Other dwellings are made of mud and wooden poles with palm leaf roofs.

In Nyeri, near Mount Kenya, Kikuyu families live in stone houses with corrugated iron roofs.

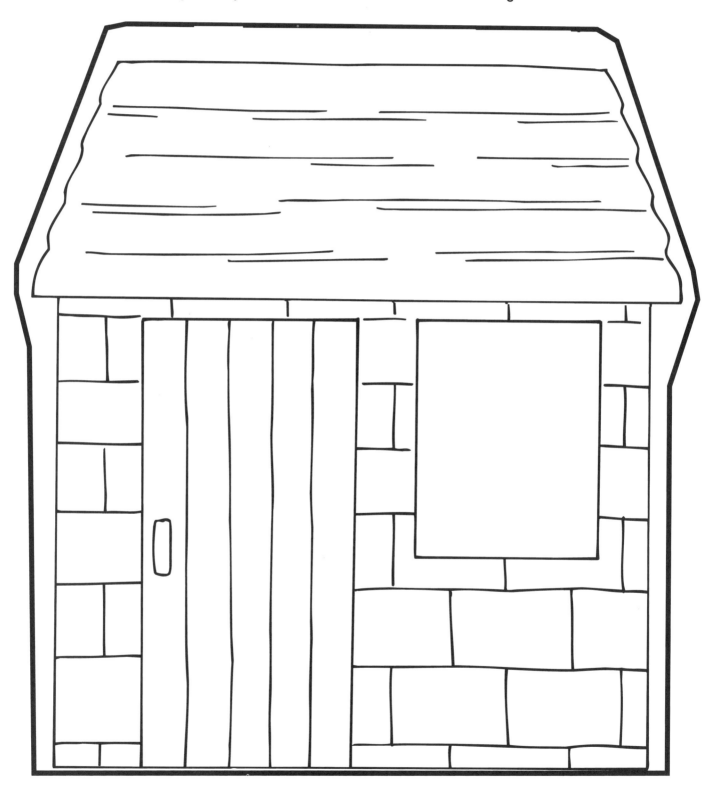

Bulletin Board Patterns: Animals of Kenya

Elephants, giraffes, lions, hippopotamuses, rhinoceroses, zebras, and many kinds of antelopes can be found in Kenya's national parks.

Bulletin Board Patterns: People of Kenya

Kenya is home to many different people with differing customs, traditions, and clothing.

In Mombasa, men wear modern short-sleeved shirts, shorts or long pants, and sandals. Young boys usually wear short-sleeved shirts and khaki shorts, and go barefoot.

Although many people wear modern clothing, there are still those who wear traditional garments.

Men and young boys sometimes wear colorful draped cloths tied around their necks.

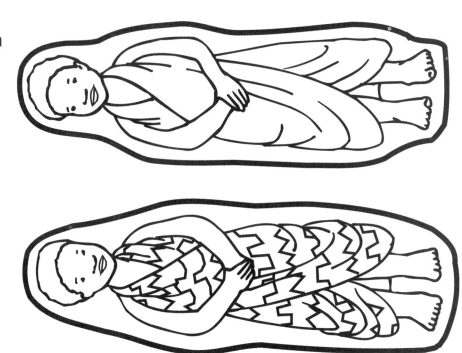

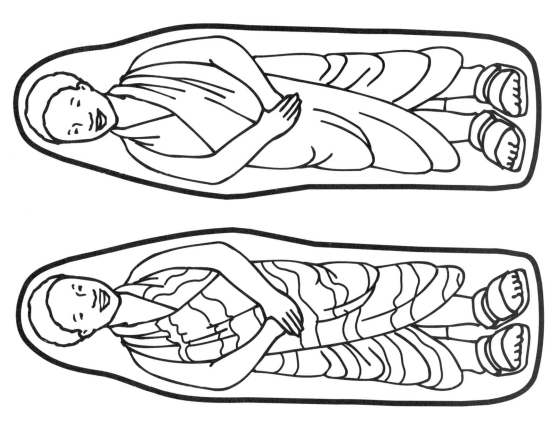

Bulletin Board Patterns: People of Kenya

Most women and young girls wear simple clothing and ornaments such as colorful headbands, necklaces, and earrings.

Some young girls wear blouses with wrap-around skirts.

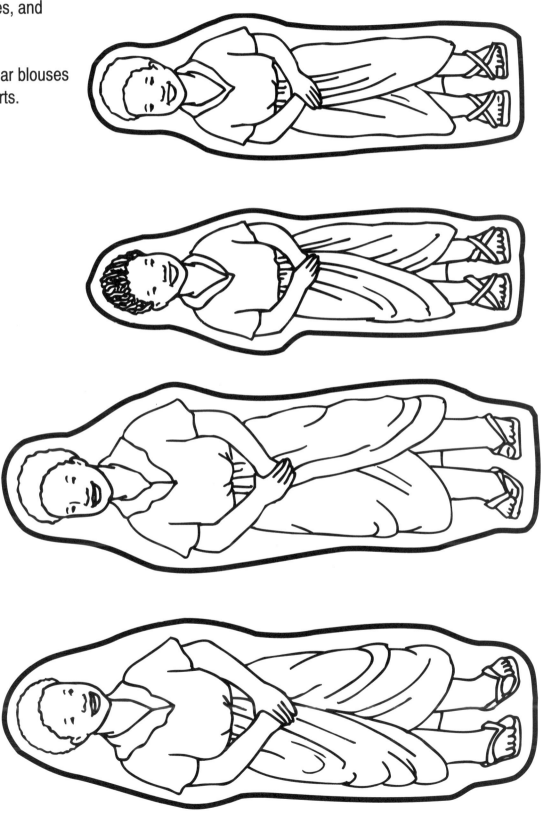

More Patterns for Kenya
Food and Tools

Corn, pineapple, sugar, wheat, and coffee are important products in Kenya.

Cornmeal mush is eaten by many people in Kenya. Another food is *irio*, which is kidney beans and hominy wrapped in banana leaves.

1. **Mbuzi**, pronounced BOO-zee, is a stool with a point on the front used to grate coconuts.
2. **Baskets** are used for carrying supplies.
3. **Grinding stones** are kept outside the home to grind corn or maize.
4. **Gourds** are used to transport water.

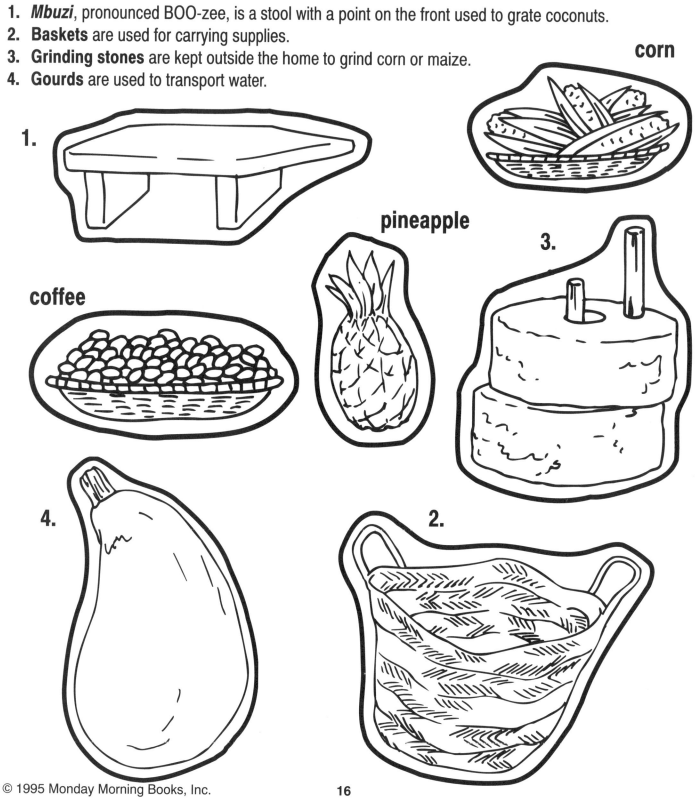

corn

pineapple

coffee

1.

3.

4.

2.

More Patterns for Kenya
Jewelry, Crafts, and Transportation

1. **Jewelry** such as necklaces, earrings, and headbands are made from shells.
2. **Wooden figurines** are carved from wild olive and ebony trees.
3. **Trucks** are used to transport products for sale in the marketplace.

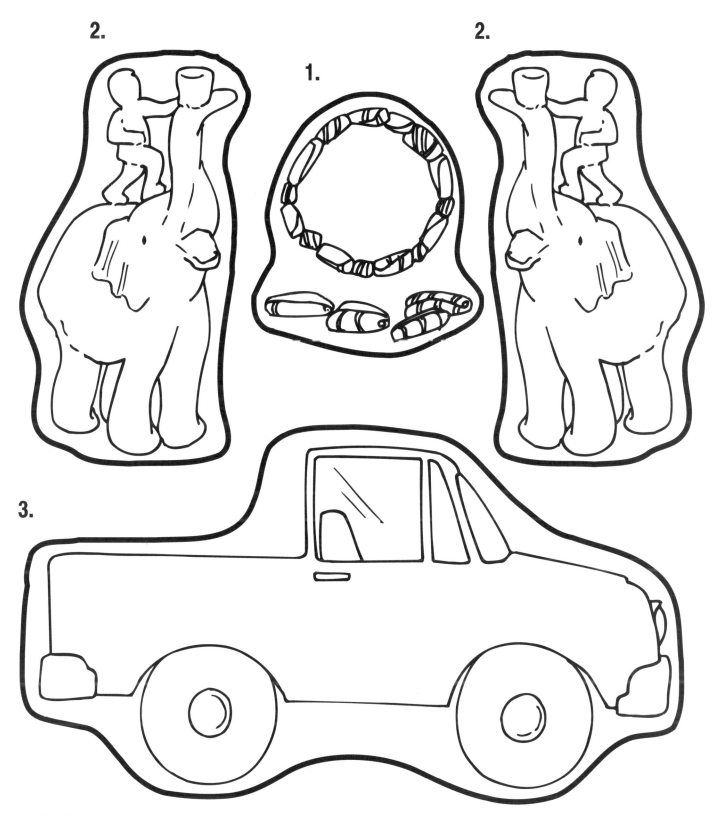

More Patterns for Kenya
Music, Games, and Landmarks

Musical Instruments

Drums are important instruments in Kenya. Drums of different shapes and sizes are made from hollowed tree trunks.

Horns of varied shapes are used during special occasions.

Flutes are made of bamboo or other hollow plants.

Games

Kigogo is a game played with round stones or dried beans. The object is for one player to take the other players' pieces. Some children prefer to play checkers.

Landmark

The Jamai Mosque is one of two mosques found in Nairobi. These structures are houses of worship for Moslem communities.

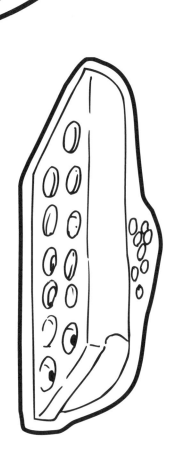

Kenyan Craft Activities

Let's Make a Kenyan Diorama

Ask each student to bring an empty shoe box to school. Provide paint and brushes for students to paint their boxes to resemble an area in Kenya.

Reproduce the patterns on pages 12-18 for students to color, cut out, and glue inside their dioramas.

When the dioramas are completed, display student projects on a table in front of your Kenyan community bulletin board.

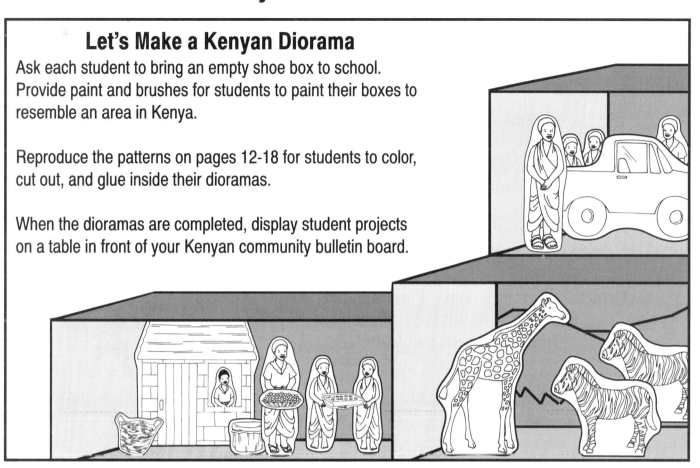

Let's Make a Safari Mobile

Provide students with the animal patterns on page 13 to use as templates. Also provide construction paper, markers, scissors, hole punch, yarn, and a 12" cardboard circle.

Have each child decorate his or her cardboard circle and punch holes around the edge. Cut lengths of yarn to attach animal patterns around the circle.

When mobiles are finished, lace and tie a length of yarn through the holes and hang from your classroom ceiling.

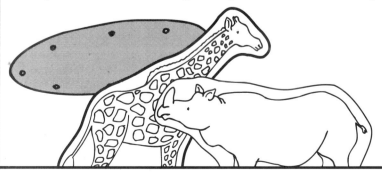

Kenyan Literature Links

Ashanti to Zulu
by Margaret Musgrove
Dial Books for Young Readers, 1976

Learn about twenty-six different African communities including the people, dwellings, animals, and artifacts.

African Picture Books
Provide children with 8" x 10" brown grocery bag pages, a variety of craft supplies, and patterns to create individual picture books about Kenya. Punch holes and bind pages with rope, twine, or yarn. Invite each student to share his or her African picture book with the class.

An African Picture Book by Stephanie Bell

More Books About Kenya and Africa

A Promise to the Sun
by Tololwa Marti Mollel, Little, Brown & Co., 1992

Abiyoyo
by Pete Seeger, Macmillan, 1986

African Crafts
by Jane Kerina, Lion Books, 1970

Beat the Story Drum, Pum-Pum
by Ashley Bryan, Atheneum Publishers, 1980

Bring the Rain to Kapiti Plain: A Nandi Tale
by Verna Aardema, Dial Books for Young Readers, 1981

Bury My Bones But Keep My Words
by Tony Fairman, Henry Holt & Co., 1992

The Fire Children
by Eric Maddern, Little, Brown & Co., 1993

How Giraffe Got Such a Long Neck and Why Rhino Is So Grumpy
by Michael Rosen, Dial Books for Young Readers, 1993

Jambo Means Hello
by Muriel Feelings, Dial Books for Young Readers, 1981

Kenya in Pictures
prepared by Geography Dept., Lerner, 1988

The Land and the People of Kenya
by Michael Maren, Lippincott, 1989

Moja Means One
by Muriel Feelings, Dial Books for Young Readers, 1971

The Orphan Boy: A Masai Story
by Tololwa Marti Mollel, Clarion Books, 1990

Princess Gorilla and a New Kind of Water;
A Mpongwe Tale
by Verna Aardema, Dial Books for Young Readers, 1988

The Story of Lightning and Thunder
by Ashley Bryan, Atheneum Publishers, 1993

Traveling to Tondo
by Verna Aardema, Alfred A. Knopf Inc., 1991

The Village of Round and Square Houses
by Ann Grifalconi, Little, Brown & Co., 1986

Map: Asia

Cambodia is a tropical country found on the Indochina peninsula of southeastern Asia.

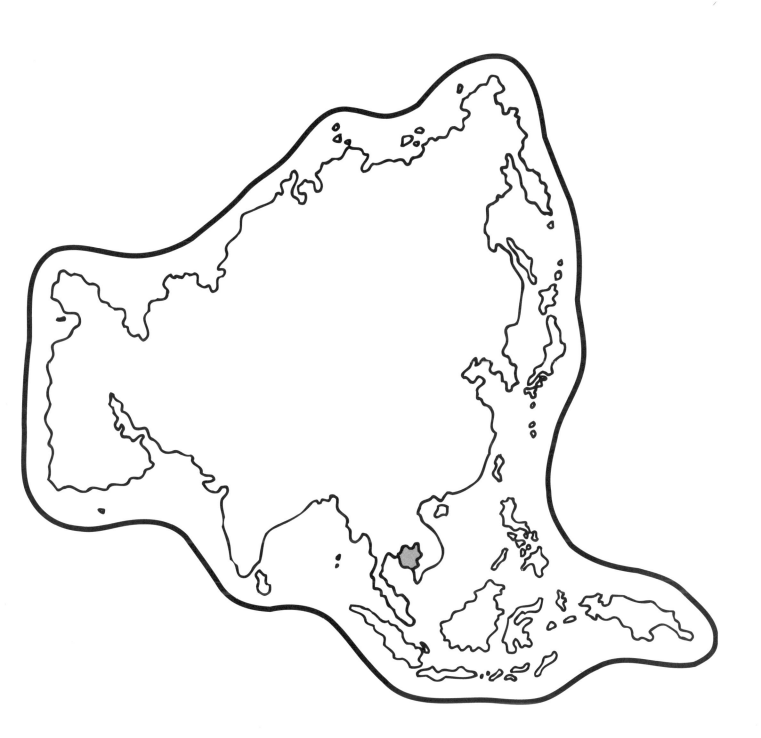

Map: Cambodia

The Mekong River is one of the longest in Asia, and Cambodia's most important.

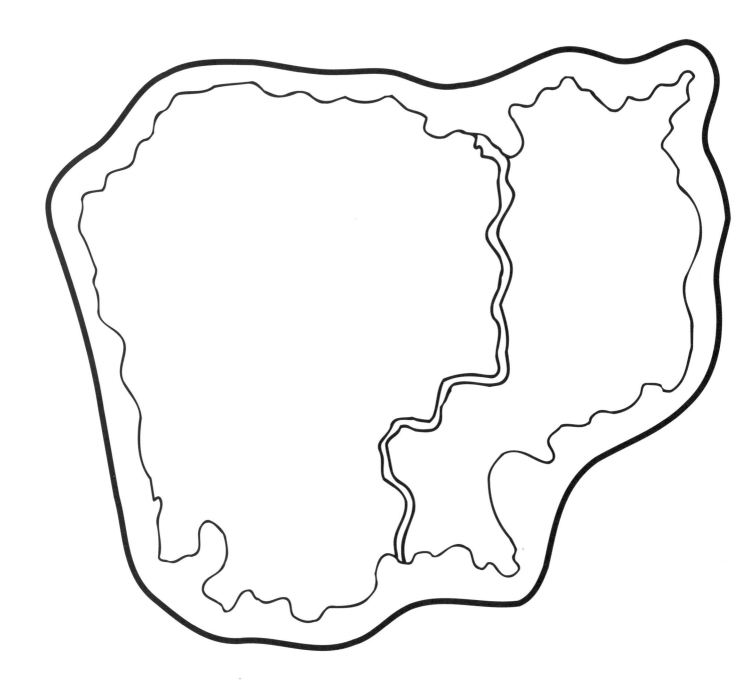

Bulletin Board: A Community in Cambodia

1. Enlarge the patterns on pages 24-30.
2. Color and cut out the patterns.
3. Cover your bulletin board with pale blue at the top of the board and green at the bottom.
4. Add an orange or yellow colored border.
5. Enlarge, color, and cut out the title below.
6. Arrange and attach the patterns to your bulletin board.

A Cambodian Community

Bulletin Board Patterns: A Dwelling in Cambodia

Many homes are built on stilts to prevent flooding during the rainy season. Traditional two- to three-room dwellings are made from wood and bamboo with thatched or tiled roofs. Modern homes of concrete are also found in Cambodian communities.

Families enter their homes by climbing ladders or stairs. Shoes are not worn indoors.

Because running water is uncommon in many Cambodian communities, each household keeps large clay jugs next to the house to collect rainwater.

Bulletin Board Patterns: Animals of Cambodia

Many farmers raise water buffalo and cows. Other animals found in Cambodia include elephants, peacocks, and snakes.

Once elephants were trained to do heavy labor. Today they have been replaced by tractors.

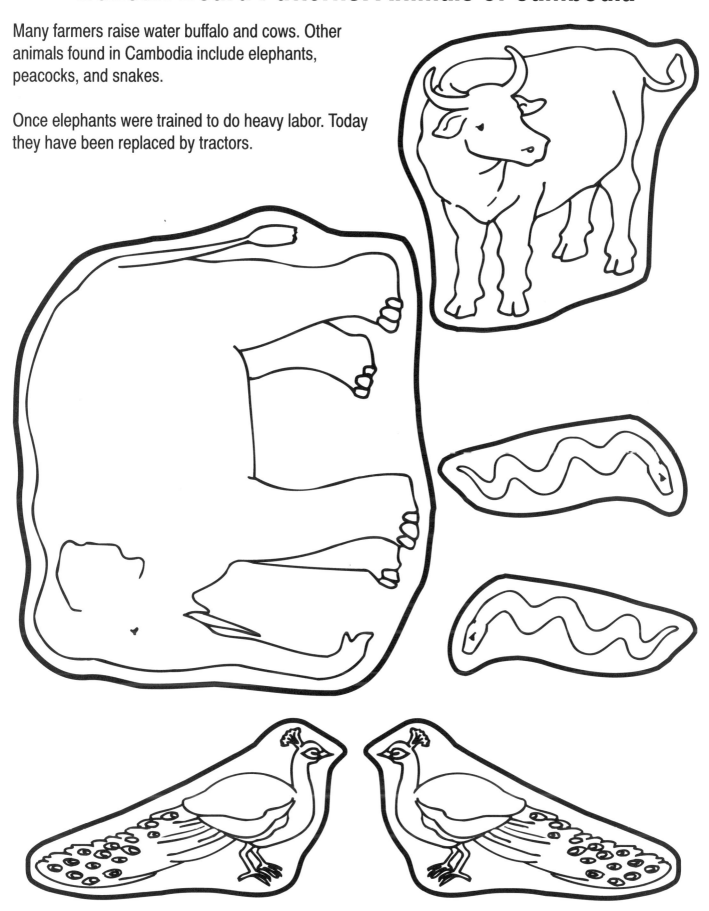

Bulletin Board Patterns: People of Cambodia

Both men and women work in the fields. Boys help with the farming as well as herd water buffalo.

A Cambodian man wears a simple *sarong*, or *krama* (a checkered scarf). To work in the fields he wears pants, a long-sleeved shirt, and a hat or scarf to protect his head from the sun.

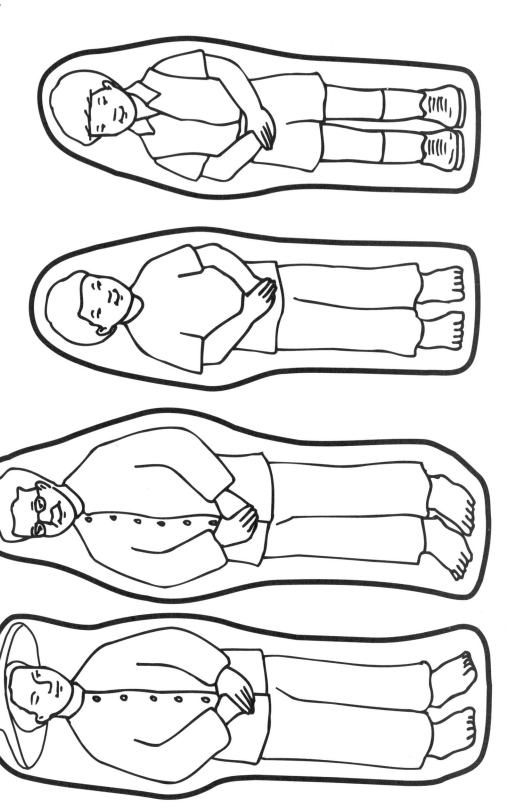

Bulletin Board Patterns: People of Cambodia

In many Cambodian communities, girls help with housework, take care of young children, and learn to weave clothing.

A Cambodian woman wears a blouse and a *sarong*. She wears a long-sleeved shirt and pants to work in the fields. She also wears a hat or scarf to protect her head from the sun.

Young women wear bright colors and bold designs. Older women wear white or black shirts and black sarongs or loose-fitting pants.

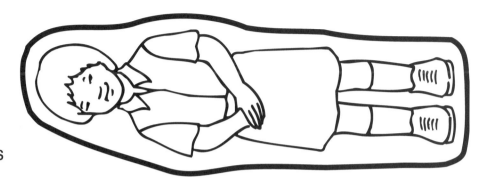

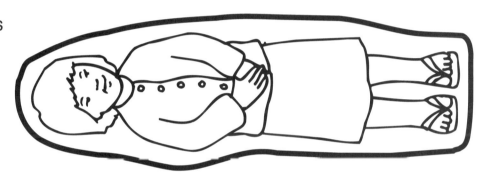

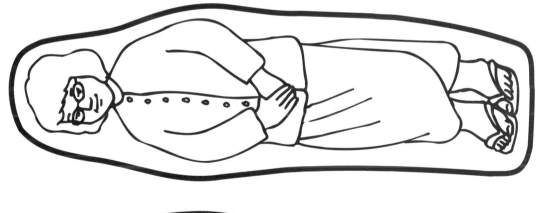

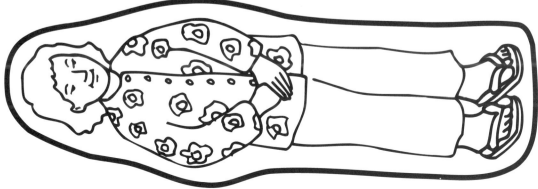

More Patterns for Cambodia
Food and Tools

Rice and rubber are the principal products of Cambodia. Other products include corn, timber, and fish.

1. **Woks** are used for cooking vegetables.
2. **Water jugs** collect rainwater.
3. **Baskets** are used for carrying supplies and serving foods.

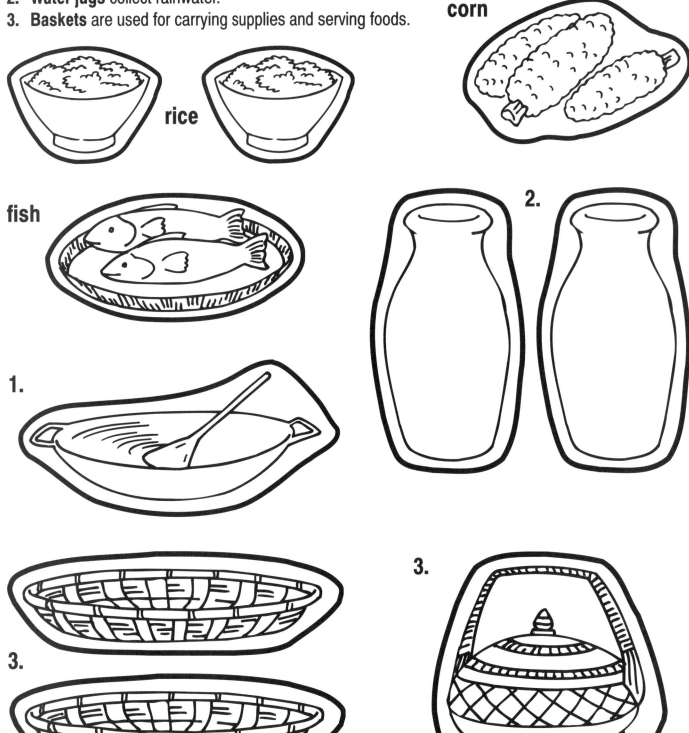

rice

corn

fish

1.

2.

3.

3.

More Patterns for Cambodia
Clothing, Crafts, and Transportation

1. *Kramas* are sarongs (scarves) worn as clothing or used to carry things.
2. **Plastic slippers** are worn when working in the fields.
3. **Shadow puppets** are used for entertainment.
4. *Cyclos* are carts used for transportation.

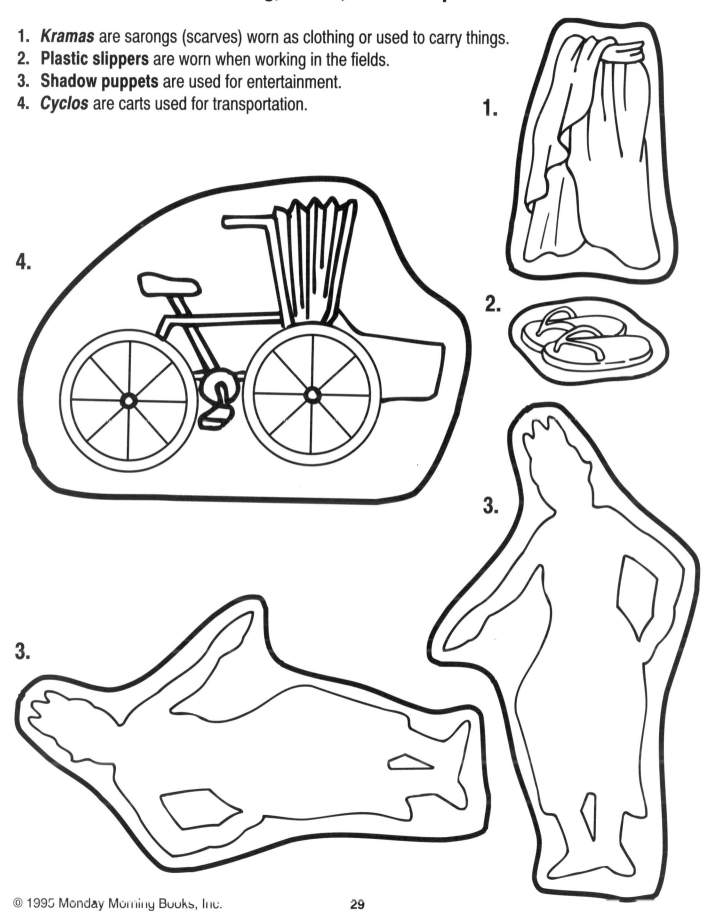

More Patterns for Cambodia
Music, Festivals, and Landmarks

Musical Instruments

Musicians in small and large orchestras play string and percussion instruments for special occasions, ceremonies, and festivals.

Water Festival

Long-boat crews race in the Water Festival during the month of November. The festival marks the change of the current of the Tonle Sap River.

Landmark

The temple of Angkor Wat in Cambodia is one of the largest religious complexes in the world. The entire structure is decorated with detailed sculptures.

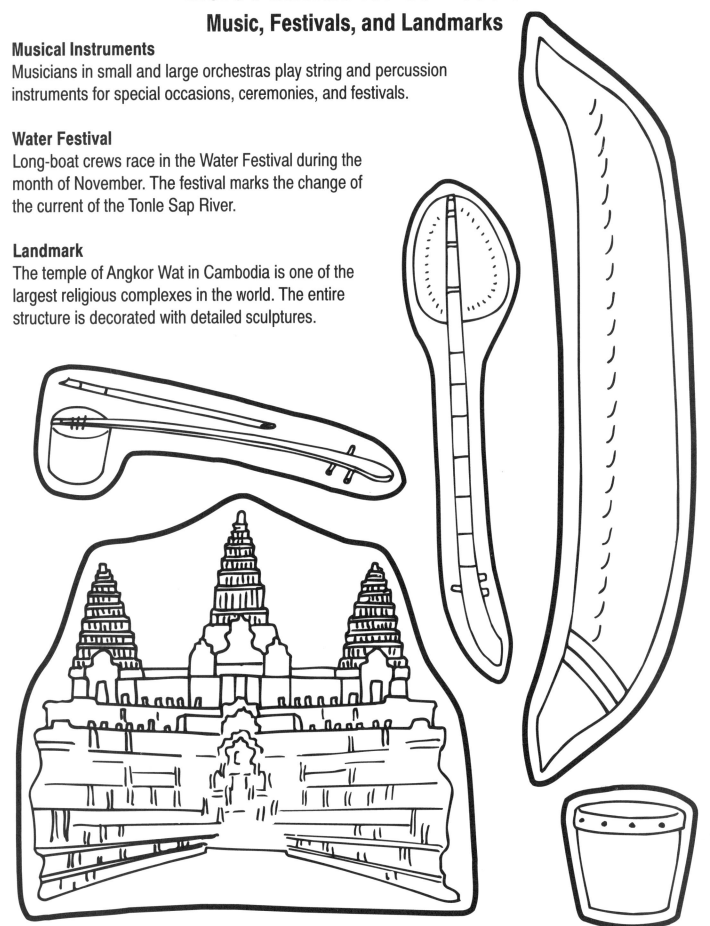

Cambodian Craft Activities

Let's Make a Cambodian Diorama

Ask each student to bring an empty shoe box to school. Provide paint and brushes for students to paint their boxes to resemble a place in Cambodia.

Reproduce the patterns on pages 24-30 for students to color, cut out, and glue inside their dioramas.

When the dioramas are completed, display student projects on a table in front of your Cambodian community bulletin board.

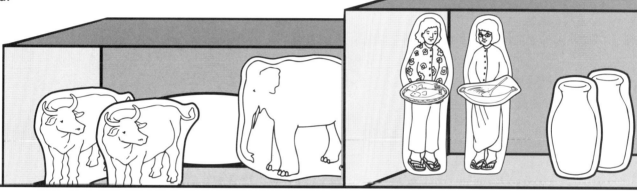

Let's Make a Water Festival Long Boat

Provide each student with two long-boat patterns (page 30), two rower patterns (below), and craft supplies.

Cut paper towel rolls in half lengthwise. Give each child a half and show how to glue a long-boat pattern to each side. Glue the rower patterns inside the boat and attach Popsicle sticks or pipe cleaners for oars.

Cambodian Literature Links

Dara's Cambodian New Year
by Sothea Chiemruom
Simon & Schuster Books, 1992

Dara, a Cambodian boy, celebrates his second New Year in the United States.

Cambodian Seascapes
Provide paint, brushes, and paper for students to paint land- or seascapes. For seascapes: show how to mix small amounts of dish detergent with paint to make foamy waves. Also provide long-boat directions and pattern (pages 30-31) for children to attach to their seascapes. For landscapes, mix sand with paints to add textured hills; use Popsicle sticks to add textured grassy plains or palm tree leaves.

More Books About Cambodia

The Clay Marble
by Minfong Ho, Farrar, Straus & Giroux, 1991

Judge Rabbit and the Tree Spirit
by Lina Mao Wall, Children's Book Press, 1991

The Land and People of Cambodia
by David P. Chandler, HarperCollins Publishers, 1991

Silent Lotus
by Jeanne M. Lee, Farrar, Straus & Giroux, 1991

Where the River Runs
by Nancy Price Graff, Little, Brown & Co., 1993

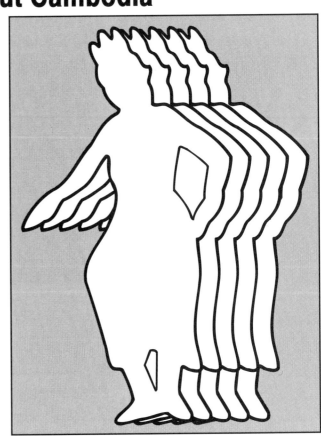

Map: Australia

Australia and New Zealand are companion states and lie in the southern part of the Pacific Ocean.

Map: New Zealand

New Zealand is made up of several islands. The three main islands are North Island, South Island, and Stewart Island.

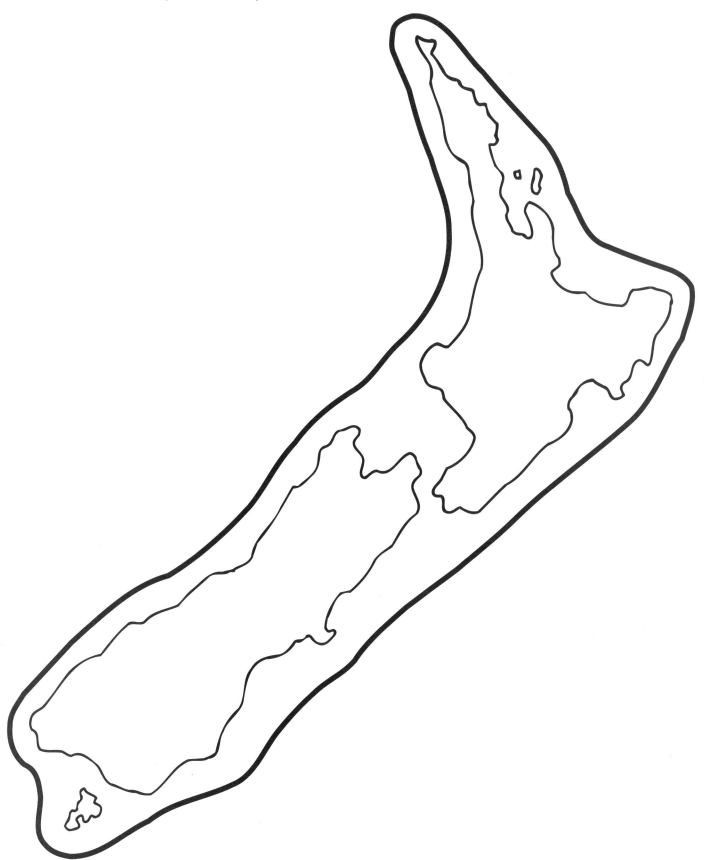

Bulletin Board: A Community in Australia

1. Enlarge the patterns on pages 36-42.
2. Color and cut out the patterns.
3. Cover your bulletin board with pale blue at the top of the board and brown or green at the bottom.
4. Add a blue or green colored border.
5. Enlarge, color, and cut out the title below.
6. Arrange and attach the patterns to your bulletin board.

An Australian Community

Bulletin Board Patterns: A Dwelling in Australia

Most homes found in Australia are one-story dwellings made of wood, with porches around one or two sides. Stone and brick houses can also be found in many communities.

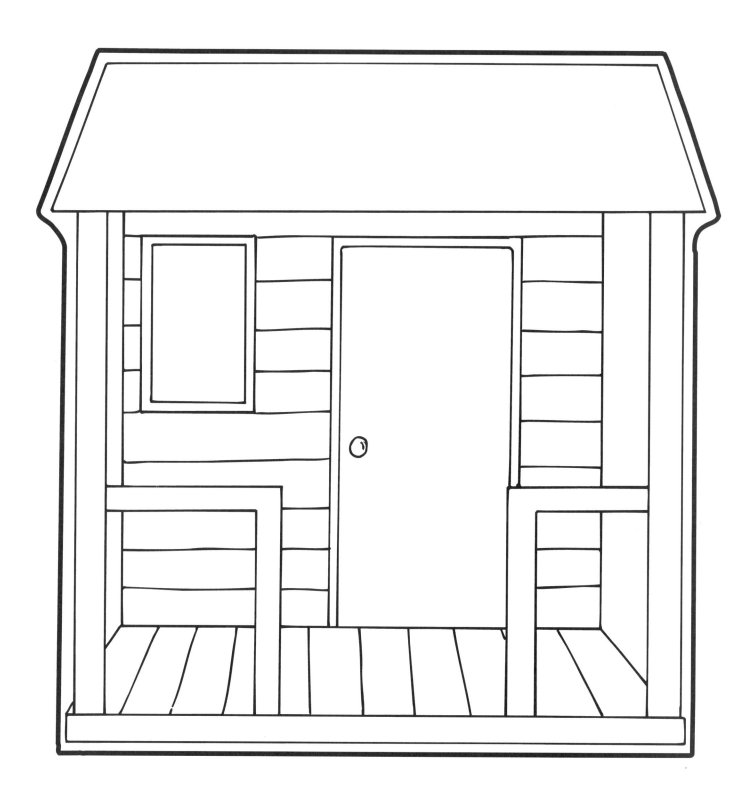

Bulletin Board Patterns: Animals of Australia

Farmers and outback ranchers raise cows and sheep. Unusual animals found in Australia and New Zealand include the kiwi and mynah birds, the tuatara (a reptile), the kangaroo, the koala, and the glow worm. Glow worms are the larvae of tiny flies and look like mosquitoes.

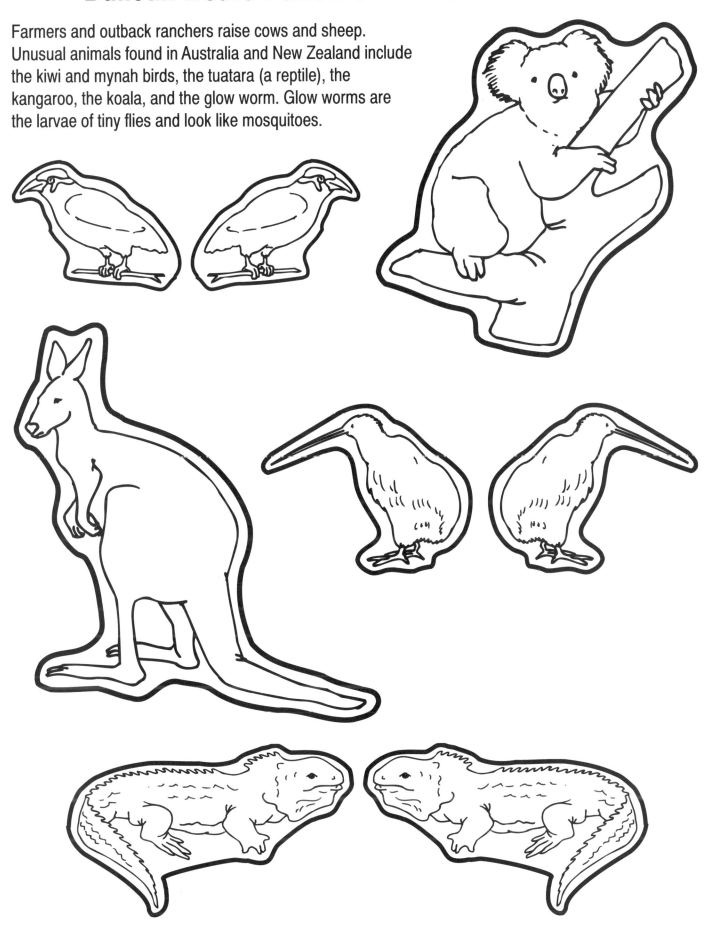

Bulletin Board Patterns: People of Australia

Today, most Australians wear modern clothing. Outback ranchers wear clothing similar to early American cowboys. Many people dress in traditional costumes for special occasions and holidays.

The Maoris are descendants of an ancient Polynesian culture who lived in New Zealand and have a history similar to Hawaiians. Their costumes are made of flax and decorated with geometric patterns. On special occasions Maoris men wear knee-length skirts and a shawl made of woven flax.

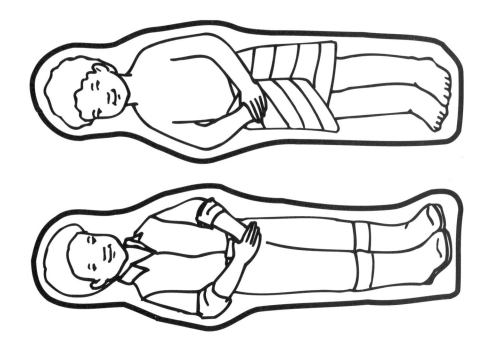

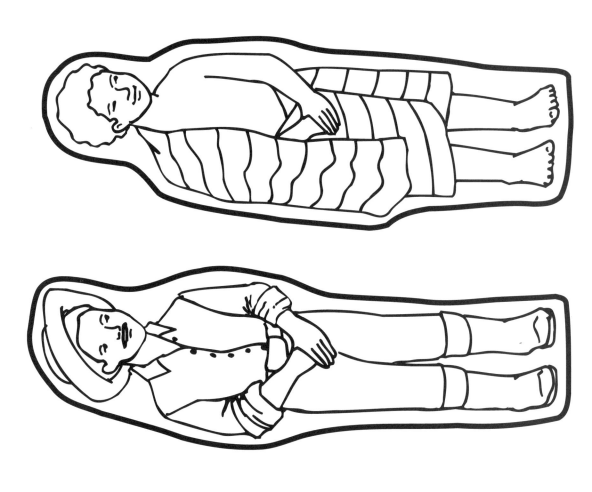

Bulletin Board Patterns: People of Australia

The women of Australia and New Zealand wear modern everyday clothing.

On special occasions Maori women perform traditional dances. They wear skirts and sleeveless blouses decorated with rectangular patterns. They also wear ornaments such as necklaces and headbands made of stone, shark teeth, and feathers.

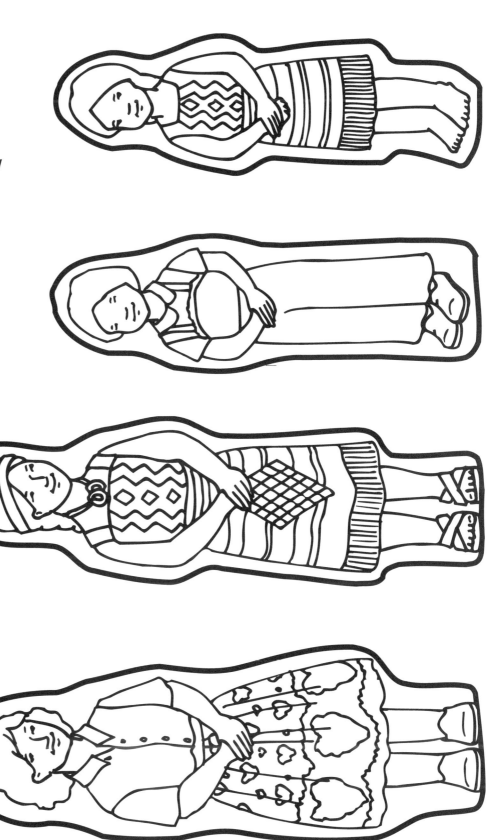

More Patterns for Australia
Food and Animals

Today, farmers in Australia raise wheat, barley, oats, fruit, and potatoes. Flounder and oysters are also important products in New Zealand.

Australia and New Zealand are one of the world's largest producers of sheep. Sheep dogs round up mobs of sheep.

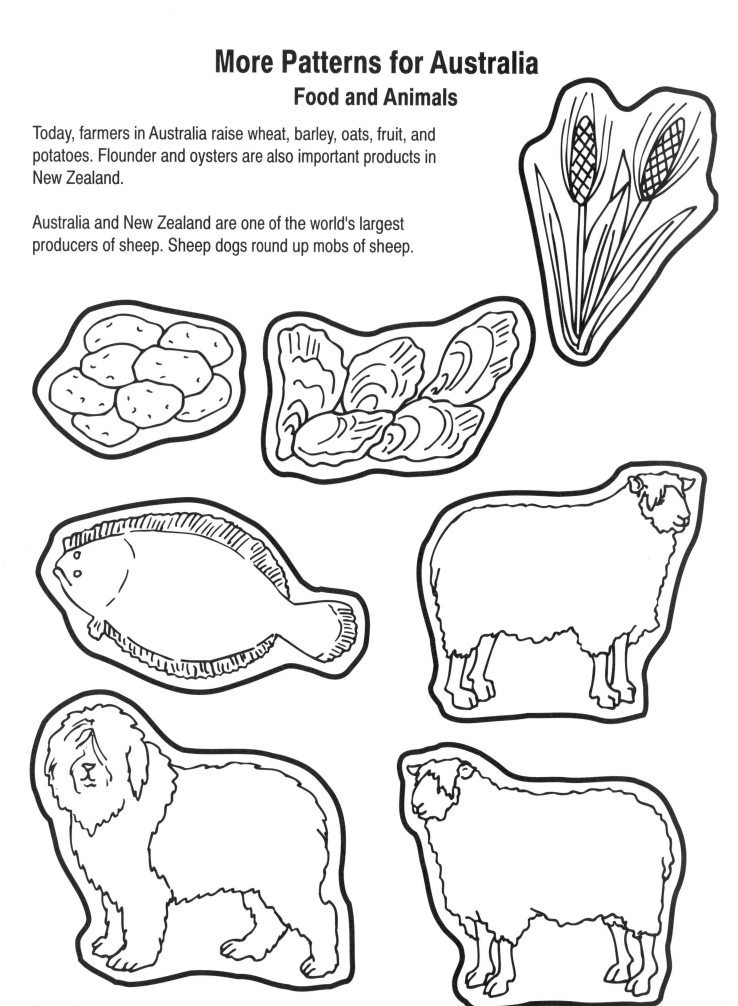

More Patterns for Australia and New Zealand
Clothing, Crafts, and Transportation

1. **Maori woodcarvings** were once used to decorate dwellings and canoes. Today, woodcarvers still practice this ancient craft.
2. **Woven flax** is used to make traditional costumes worn on special occasions.
3. **Automobiles** provide transportation in most areas. Small planes are often used to spread fertilizer.

1.

1.

2.

1.

3.

More Patterns for Australia
Landmarks

The Opera House in Sydney and the Parliament buildings found in Wellington, New Zealand, are examples of the area's unique modern architectural design.

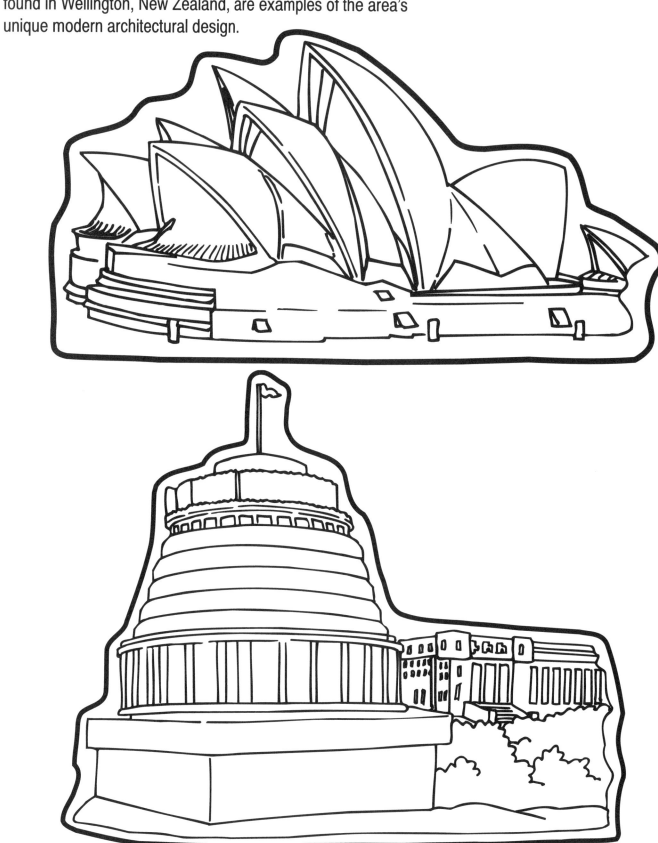

Australian Craft Activities

Let's Make an Australian Diorama

Ask each student to bring an empty shoe box to school. Provide paint and brushes for students to paint their boxes to resemble a place in Australia.

Reproduce the patterns on pages 36-42 for students to color, cut out, and glue inside their dioramas.

When the dioramas are completed, display student projects on a table in front of your Australian community bulletin board.

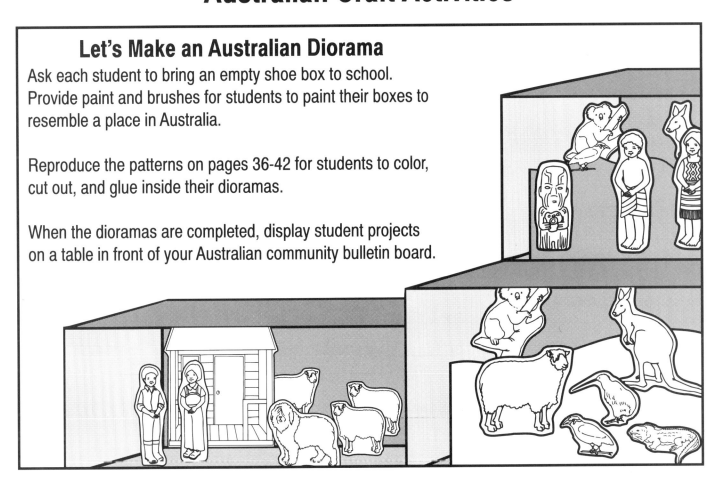

Let's Make a Maori Carving

Provide students with drying clay, brown paint, and carving tools. Then show them how to make slabs or cylinder-shaped clay forms to carve.

Make a slab by pinching a ball of clay into a rectangle, square, or free-form shape. Use a rolling pin to refine the slab by gently rolling the pin from the center out to the edges. Or, roll a ball of clay into a thick cylindrical shape.

Allow forms to dry until leather hard. Then show students how to carve designs with plastic knives, old ballpoint pens, teaspoons, Popsicle sticks, or large paper clips.

Note: To slow drying, cover slabs and cylinders with damp paper towels and cover loosely with a plastic bag. Do not seal the bag. Check dryness daily.

Australian Literature Links

Shoes from Grandpa
by Mem Fox
Orchard Books, 1990

Family members describe clothing to go with Jessie's shoes from Grandpa.

Crafty Clothes
Provide students with colored construction paper to create a festive wardrobe for a paper doll. Show how to tear, fold, and glue construction paper scraps to make a variety of clothing. For example: show how to cut fringe for a woolly coat or trim for a dress or show how to crumple, then flatten brown construction paper for a leather coat.

More Books About Australia and New Zealand

A Little Fear
by Patricia Wrightson, Atheneum Publishers, 1983

Balyet
by Patricia Wrightson, McElderry Books, 1989

The Bamboo Flute
by Garry Disher, Ticknor & Fields, 1993

The Champion
by Maurice Gee, Simon & Schuster, 1993

Down Under: Vanishing Cultures
by Jan Reynolds, Harcourt Brace Jovanovich, 1992

Eleanor, Elizabeth
by Libby Gleeson, Holiday House, 1990

Enemies
by Robin Klein, Dutton, 1989

Farmer Shulz's Ducks
by Collin Thiele, Harper & Row, 1988

The Good Fortunes Gang
by Margaret Mahy, Delacorte Press, 1993

Hattie and the Fox
by Mem Fox, Bradbury Press, 1987

Koala Lou
by Mem Fox, Harcourt Brace Jovanovich, 1989

The Maoris
by Charles Higham, Lerner, 1983

The Nargun and the Stars
by Patricia Wrightson, McElderry Books, 1986

New Zealand in Pictures
prepared by the Geography Dept., Lerner, 1990

Night Noises
by Mem Fox, Harcourt Brace Jovanovich, 1989

Playing Beatie Bow
by Ruth Park, Antheneum, 1982

Shadow Shark
by Collin Thiele, Harper & Row, 1988

Where the Forest Meets the Trees
by Jeannie Baker, Greenwillow Books, 1988

Map: Europe

Spain occupies most of the Iberian Peninsula. It is separated from the rest of Europe by the Pyrenees Mountains.

45

Map: Spain

In Spanish, Spain is called España. The people of this country have been conquered by ancient Romans, Germanic tribes, the Moors, and many others.

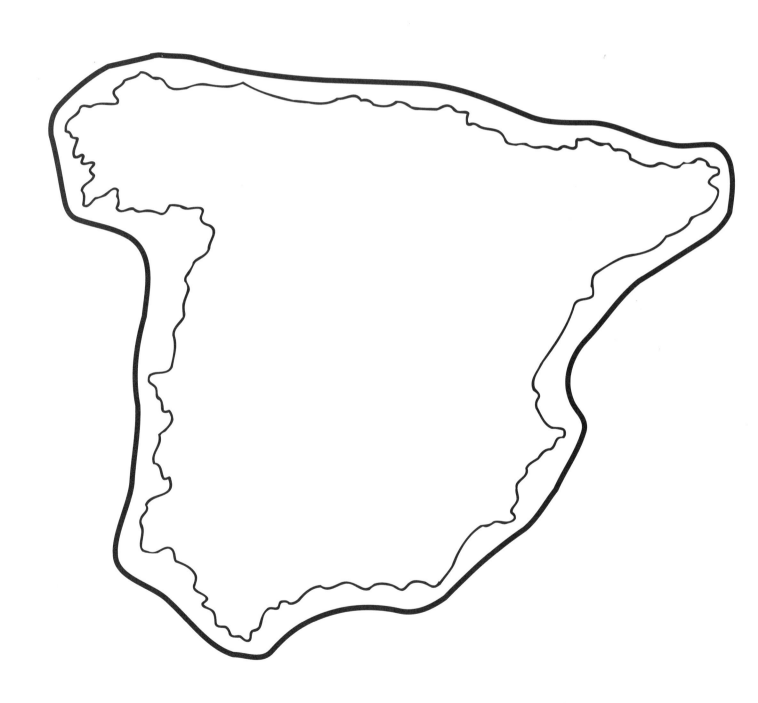

Bulletin Board: A Community in Spain

1. Enlarge the patterns on pages 48-54.
2. Color and cut out the patterns.
3. Cover your bulletin board with pale blue at the top of the board and green at the bottom.
4. Add a red colored border.
5. Enlarge, color, and cut out the title below.
6. Arrange and attach the patterns to your bulletin board.

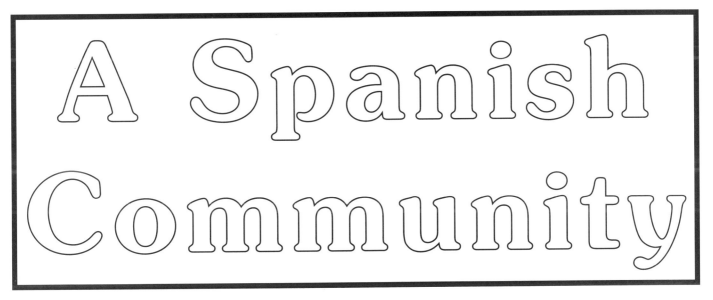

Bulletin Board Patterns: A Dwelling in Spain

Dwellings in Spain are usually made of brick or stone with iron grillwork in the windows. Some homes are also whitewashed.

Bulletin Board Patterns: Animals of Spain

Animals found in Spain's wilderness include foxes, wolves, rabbits, goats, deer, and boars.

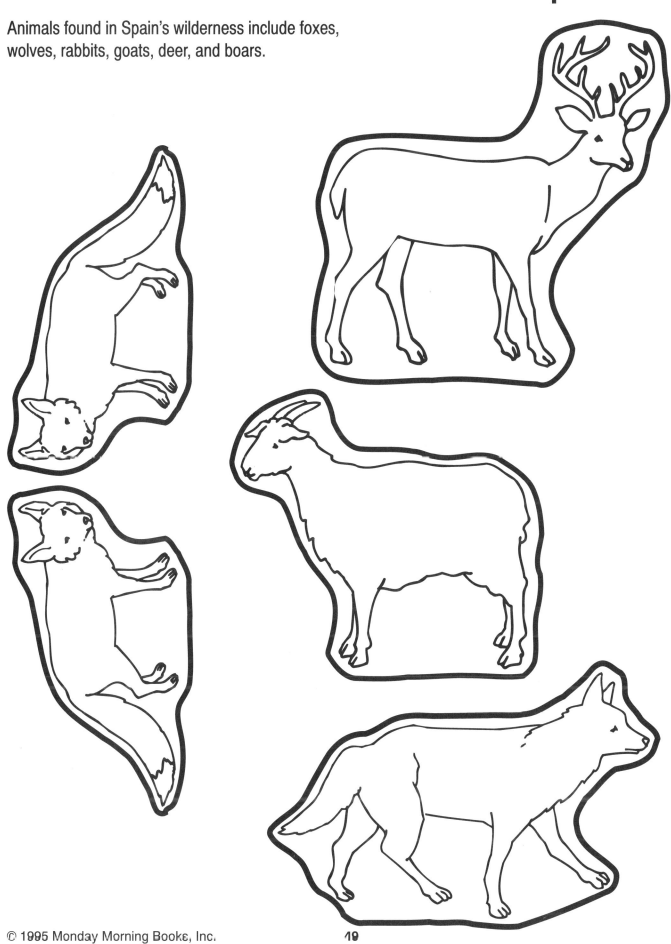

Bulletin Board Patterns: People of Spain

Men, women, and children wear modern clothing. However, in each region traditional costumes are worn to celebrate special occasions.

In Andalusia a man's special-occasion costume is knee-length pants, a short jacket, a beret, a *faja* (wide belt), flat shoes, and stockings.

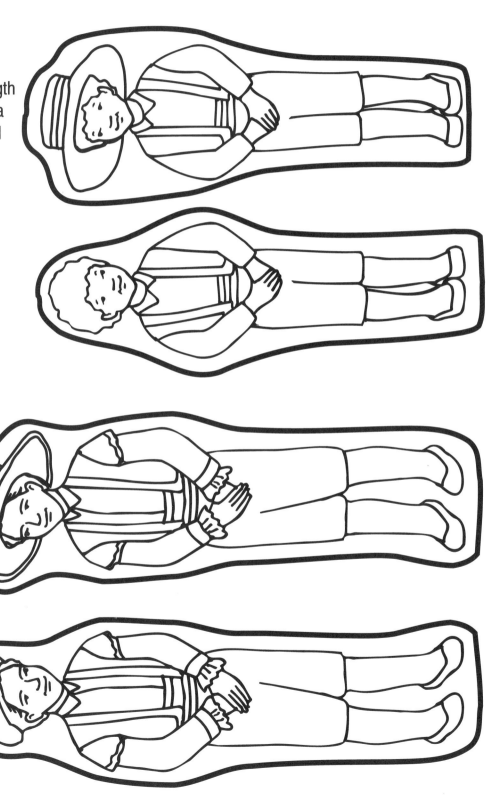

Bulletin Board Patterns: People of Spain

A woman in Andalusia wears a traditional strapless dress with a flowing skirt, a brightly decorated scarf or shawl called a *mantilla*, high-heel shoes, and an ornamental comb in her hair.

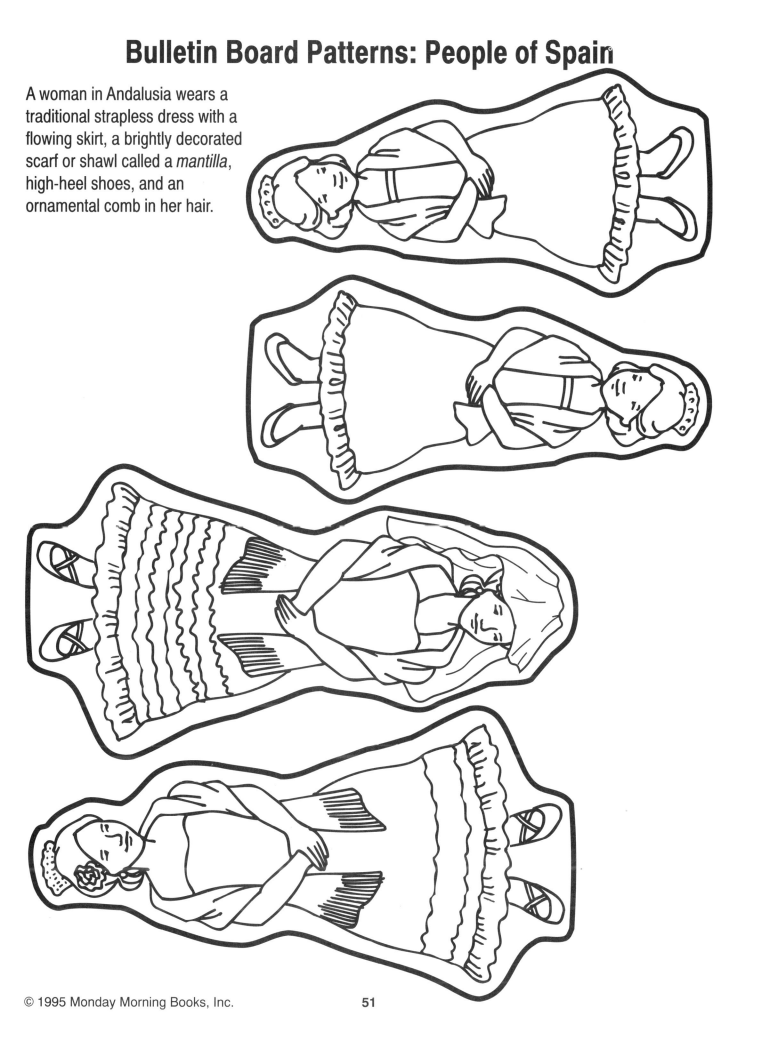

51

More Patterns for Spain
Food and Transportation

Wheat is the main product of Spain. Farmers also raise sheep and cotton. Corn, olives, oranges, lemons, figs, and almonds are also grown in different regions of the country.

1. *Paella* is a favorite food of Spain, a seafood dish combining rice, saffron, lobster, shrimp, chicken, vegetables, eel, squid, and crab.
2. **Carts** drawn by donkeys or oxen are used to transport supplies.

1.

almonds   **lemons**   **corn**

oranges   **olives**

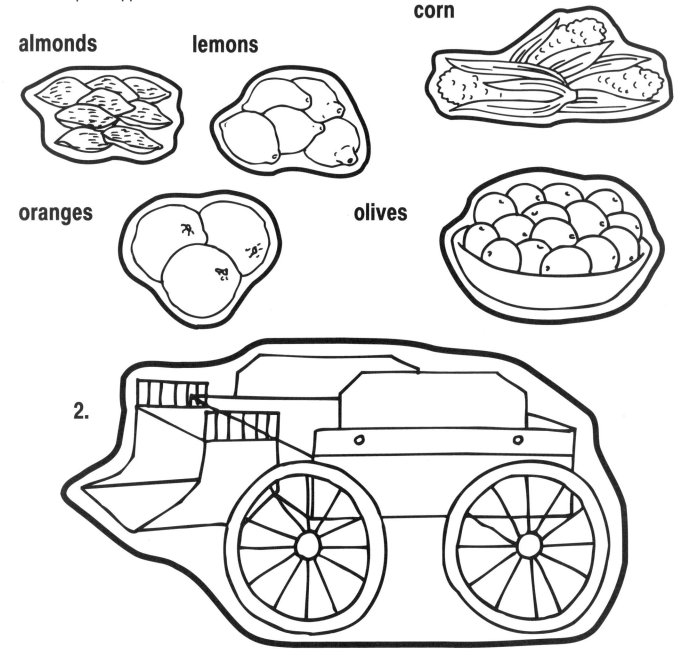

2.

More Patterns for Spain
Arts and Tools

1. **Lace** is made in Valencia and sold in the marketplace.
2. **Fishing gear** including a rope, basket, a wooden box, and oars is important in north-central Spain.

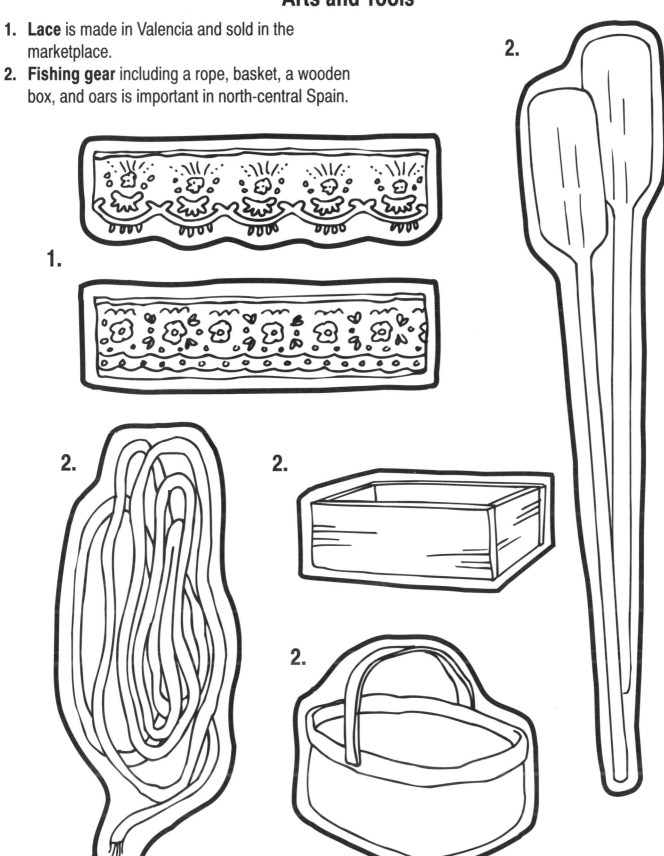

1.

2.

2.

2.

2.

More Patterns for Spain
Music, Festivals, and Landmarks

Musical Instruments

Guitars, tambourines, castanets, and *gaitas* (Spanish bagpipes) are popular instruments in Spain.

Sanfermines Festival

This is the largest and noisiest festival in Spain. The half-mile run that is part of it takes place through the streets of Pamplona, ending at the bullfighting ring.

Landmark

The storybook castle called Alcazár was built in 1358 in Old Castile in Segovia. The famous Queen Isabella of Castille was coronated in the castle in 1474, 18 years before helping Christopher Columbus.

Spanish Craft Activities

Let's Make a Spanish Diorama

Ask each student to bring an empty shoe box to school. Provide paint and brushes for students to paint their boxes to resemble a place in Spain.

Reproduce the patterns on pages 48-54 for students to color, cut out, and glue inside their dioramas.

When the dioramas are completed, display student projects on a table in front of your Spanish community bulletin board.

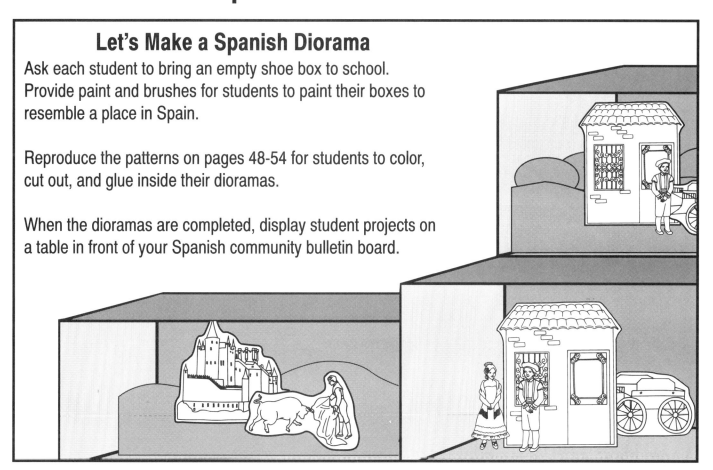

Let's Make a Spanish Castle

Ask children to bring paper towel and toilet paper rolls, paper cups, shoe boxes, and a variety of small gift boxes to school.

Also provide students with crayons, construction paper, markers, scissors, glue, and other craft materials to create their own storybook castles. Provide each child with a copy of the castle on page 54 to use as an example.

Ask students to write a story about their castle, then display finished castles and stories on a table in your classroom.

Spanish Literature Links

The Story of Ferdinand
by Munro Leaf

Ferdinand, a gentle bull, likes to smell flowers rather than fight in the bull ring.

A Garden for Ferdinand
Transform your classroom into Ferdinand's flower garden. Provide students with construction paper and a large, empty plastic soda bottle with the top cut off. Have children decorate soda bottles with construction paper flowers. Fill containers with potting soil for students to plant flowering seeds. Enlarge, color, and cut out a black construction paper bull and position it near the flower garden.

More Books About Spain

Bridle the Wind
  by Joan Aiken, Delacorte Press, 1983
Esteban the Ghost
  by Sibyl Hancock, Delacorte Press, 1983
Let's Go/Vamos: A Book in Two Languages
  by Rebecca Emberley, Little, Brown & Co., 1993
More Fun in Spanish
  by Lee Pelham Cooper, Little, Brown & Co., 1967
My Day/Mi Día: A Book in Two Languages
  by Rebecca Emberley, Little, Brown & Co., 1993
My House/Mi Casa: A Book in Two Languages
  by Rebecca Emberley, Little, Brown & Co., 1970
Shadow of a Bull
  by Maia Wojciechowski, Atheneum Publishers, 1964

Spain
  edited by MaryLee Knowlton & Mark J. Sacher, Gareth Stevens Publishers, 1987
Taking a Walk/Caminado: A Book in Two Languages
  by Rebecca Emberley, Little, Brown & Co., 1970

Map: North America

The Hopis are believed to have begun one of the two oldest settlements of pueblo dwellers in North America.

Map: Hopi Territory

This map shows the approximate southwestern territory of Native Americans. The Hopis occupied an area in what is known today as Arizona.

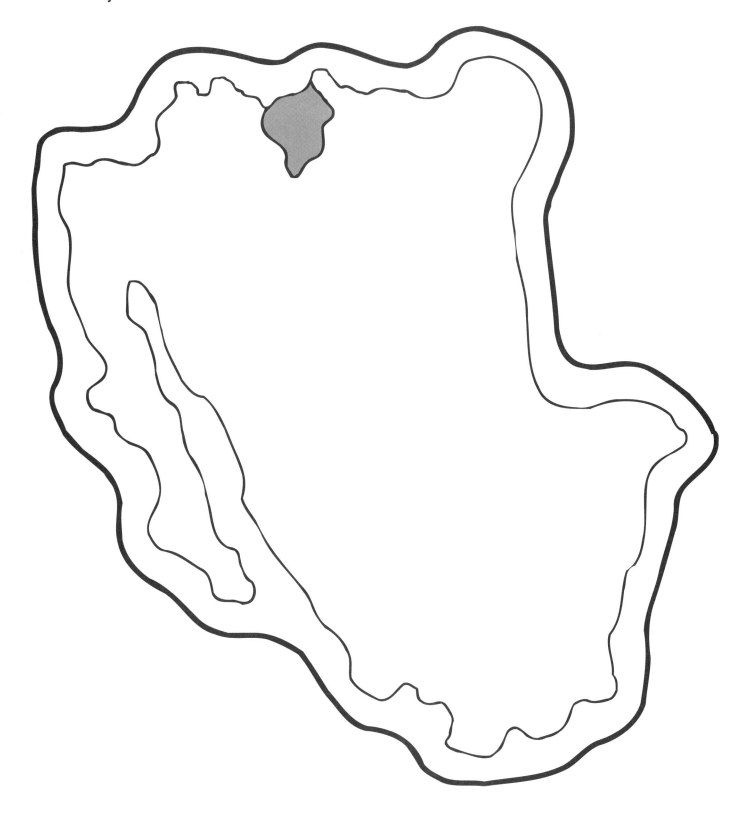

Bulletin Board: A Hopi Community

1. Enlarge the patterns on pages 60-66.
2. Color and cut out the patterns.
3. Cover your bulletin board with pale blue at the top of the board and brown or green at the bottom.
4. Add an orange or rust colored border.
5. Enlarge, color, and cut out the title below.
6. Arrange and attach the patterns to your bulletin board.

59

Bulletin Board Patterns: A Hopi Dwelling

The Hopis lived in communities of multi-chamber structures. These structures were built of stone and covered with mud plaster. A Hopi family lived in a one-room dwelling that was divided into work and storage areas, and slept on the smooth clay floor.

Each community also had one or more *kivas.* A kiva was an underground room used by the men of the village as a clubhouse and for council meetings. It was also used as a weavers' workshop. Each man belonged to only one kiva.

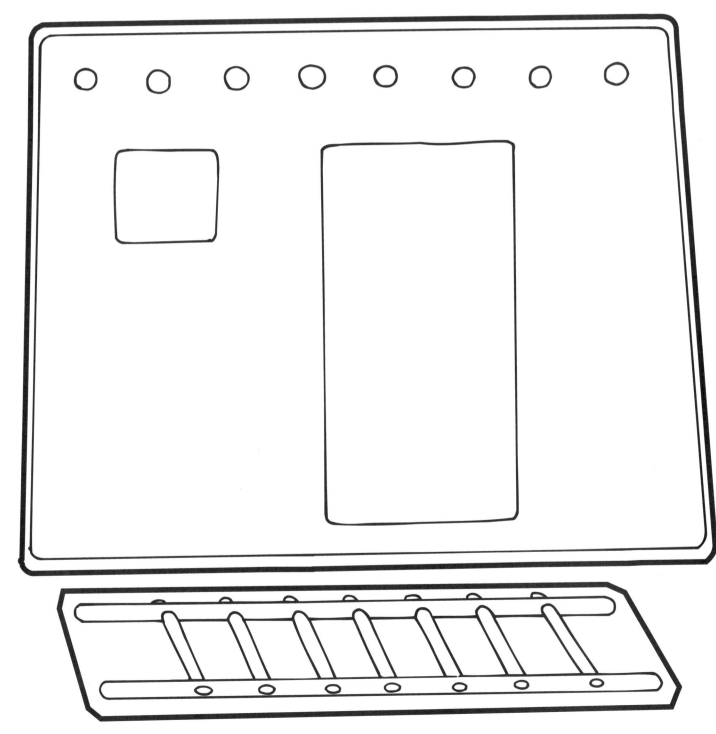

Bulletin Board Patterns: Animals of a Hopi Community

The Hopi raised sheep for wool. They also raised other livestock and kept certain birds for feathers to use as decorations.

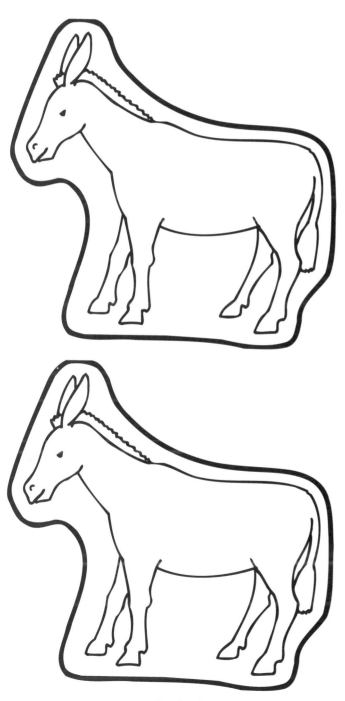

Bulletin Board Patterns: People of a Hopi Community

The Hopi men did all the weaving. Unlike other Native Americans, the Hopis' clothing was made of woven cloth. The men also made jewelry of silver and turquoise.

A Hopi man wore a headband, a woven blanket over his shoulders, jewelry and a belt decorated with silver and turquoise, and ankle-length moccasins.

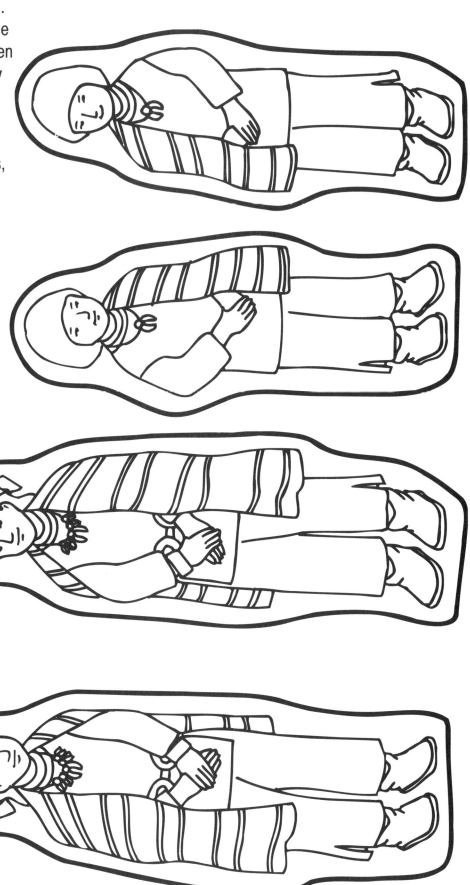

Bulletin Board Patterns: People of a Hopi Community

Hopi women ground corn, prepared meals, wove baskets, and made pottery. Pottery-making skills were taught to daughters by their mothers.

The Hopi woman wore a *manta* or one-shoulder dress over a white blouse. She also wore a woven sash and white moccasins with matching legging wraps.

Hopi girls wore a special hairstyle known as a squash blossom hairdo when they grew up. They had to show their skills by grinding corn for four days before they could have their hair fashioned into the traditional squash blossom designs.

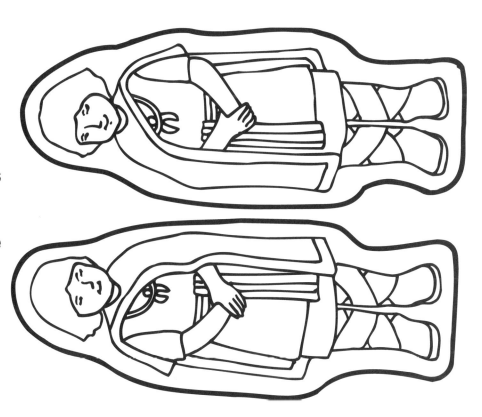

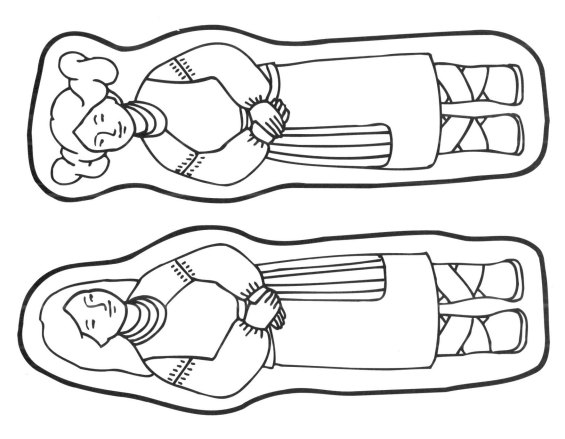

More Patterns for a Hopi Community
Food and Tools

Hopi communities grew corn, squash, beans, and tobacco. Crops received water from underground moisture. When corn was harvested, some was eaten right away, some was stored, and some was ground into cornmeal.

corn   **coffee**   **squash**

Each Hopi family had several *metates*, stone slabs of varied roughness, and a *mano*, an oblong grinding stone. The varying metates were used to grind corn into finer meal.

1. **Metates and manos** were used for grinding corn into meal.
2. **Baskets** were used for serving food.
3. **Wooden tongs** were used for picking cactus fruit.
4. **Wooden paddles** were used for making bread.
5. **Pump drills** were used for making jewelry.
6. **Spindles** with wooden whorls were used for spinning wool thread.
7. **Throwing clubs** were used for hunting small game.
8. **Trays** were used for serving food.
9. **Pottery** was used for serving and storage.

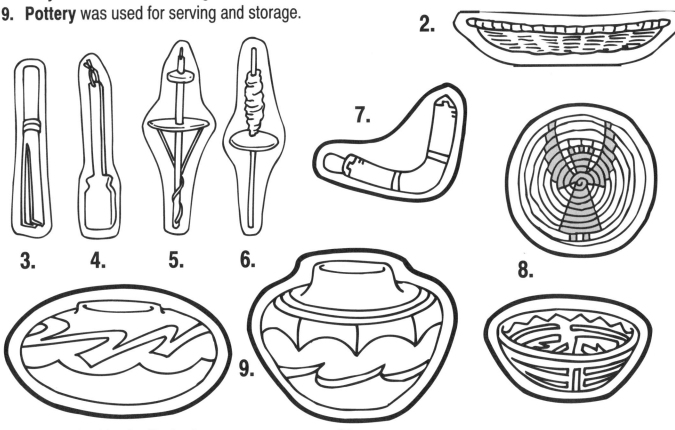

More Patterns for a Hopi Community
Clothing, Crafts, and Symbols

Kachina Dolls

Kachinas were beings that held special meaning in Hopi communities. Ceremonies were held to honor these beings and children were given kachina dolls as special gifts. These dolls were short wooden figurines and were not intended as playthings. They were used to help children learn to identify the different kachinas and what each represented.

kachina dolls

1. **Woman's moccasins** with leggings
2. **Man's moccasins**
3. **Necklace**
4. **Ceremonial sash**
5. **Buckle**
6. **Bracelet**

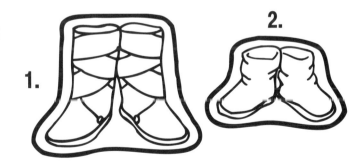

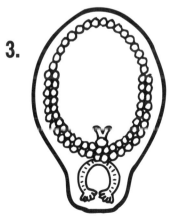

More Patterns for a Hopi Community
Music and Landmarks

Gourd Rattle
A rattle was made from a dried, carved, and decorated gourd.

Wooden Bull-Roarer
A bull-roarer was a flat, egg-shaped piece of wood. A length of leather was tied through a hole in the narrow end. When the instrument was whirled above the player's head, it made a whirring noise.

Belled Flageolet
A belled flageolet was a small wood flute.

Landmark
The Pueblo of Taos lies in the northernmost territory of pueblo dwellers. Families still live in this multi-chambered community that was built in the 1700s.

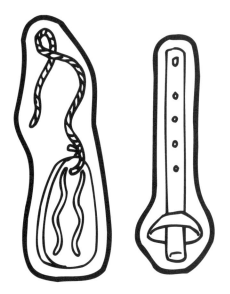

Hopi Craft Activities

Let's Make a Hopi Diorama

Ask each student to bring an empty shoe box to school. Provide paint and brushes for students to paint their boxes to resemble a Hopi location.

Reproduce the patterns on pages 60-66 for students to color, cut out, and glue inside their dioramas.

When the dioramas are completed, display student projects on a table in front of your Hopi community bulletin board.

Let's Make a Hopi Necklace

Provide a variety of macaroni noodles, paint, brushes, the patterns below, and yarn for students to make their own Hopi jewelry. Include turquoise and silver paint for decorating.

Have children paint their macaroni noodles and allow to dry. Provide crayons or markers and scissors for students to color and cut out the jewelry patterns.

Cut an 18" length of yarn for each student and have him or her string the colored macaroni and cut-out jewelry patterns. When each is done, tie a knot to make a necklace.

Hopi Literature Links

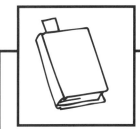

The Village of Blue Stone
by Stephen Trimble
Macmillan Publishing Co., 1990

Follow the day-to-day social life of ancient pueblo dwellers throughout a full year.

Coil, Slab, and Pinch Pots
Provide clay, brushes, and tempera paint for students to make pottery to display in the classroom. Show how to build pots using one of the following methods.

Coil method
1. Form a clay ball.
2. Roll the ball into a snake.
3. Tightly coil the first layer for bottom of pot.
4. Attach additional coil layers to form a pot. Secure coils by pinching and spreading the coils on the inside of the pot.

Slab method
1. Form a clay ball.
2. Flatten and roll the clay into a slab.
3. Cut five equal-sized squares from the slab.
4. Assemble the squares to form a pot. Secure seams by pinching the corners of each square.

Pinch method
1. Form a clay ball.
2. Using both hands, hold the ball and pinch a hole in the center with your thumbs.
3. Continue turning, pinching around the hole to form a round pot.

More Books About the Hopi and Other Native Americans

The Ancient Cliff Dwellers of Mesa Verde
by Caroline Arnold, Clarion Books, 1992

Arrow to the Sun; A Pueblo Indian Tale
by Gerald McDermott, Viking Press, 1974

Children of Clay; A Family of Pueblo Potters
by Rina Swentzell, Lerner, 1992

Children of the Earth and Sky
by Stephen Krensky, Scholastic, Inc., 1991

The Hopi
by Ann Heinrichs Tomchek, Children's Press, 1987

Island of the Blue Dolphin
by Scott O'Dell, Houghton Mifflin, 1990

The Pueblo
by Charlotte Yue, Houghton Mifflin, 1986

Quail Song
by Valerie Scho Carey, Putnam's, 1990

Sing Down the Moon
by Scott O'Dell, Houghton Mifflin, 1970

Streams to the River, River to the Sea:
A Novel of Sacajawea
by Scott O'Dell, Houghton Mifflin, 1976

When Clay Sings
by Byrd Baylor, Scribner's, 1972

Zia
by Scott O'Dell, Houghton Mifflin, 1976

Map: South America

Brazil is the largest country in South America. It is almost as large as the United States.

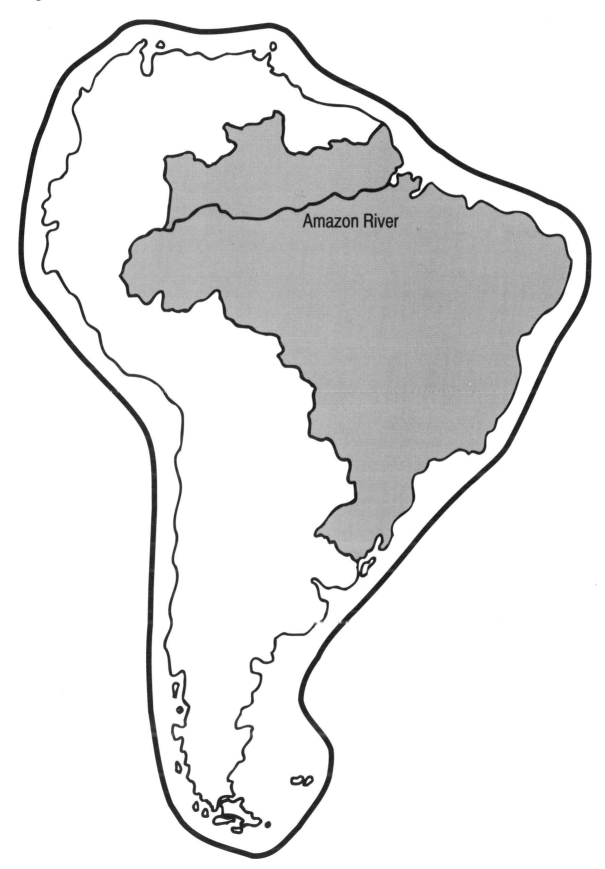

Amazon River

Map: Brazil

The Amazon River flows through Brazil. It is the longest river in the Western Hemisphere.

Amazon River

Bulletin Board: A Community in Brazil

1. Enlarge the patterns on pages 72-78.
2. Color and cut out the patterns.
3. Cover your bulletin board with pale blue at the top of the board and brown or green at the bottom.
4. Add a red, blue, or purple colored border.
5. Enlarge, color, and cut out the title below.
6. Arrange and attach the patterns to your bulletin board.

A Brazilian Community

Bulletin Board Patterns: A Dwelling in Brazil

Most Brazilians live in modern homes. Many families live in scattered communities called *favelas*. The dwellings in these favelas are small brick or stucco structures.

Bulletin Board Patterns: Animals of Brazil

Monkeys, armadillos, butterflies, birds, and giant anteaters can be found in the Amazonian forest. The Amazon River is home to manatees, turtles, stingrays, and over 700 different kinds of fish.

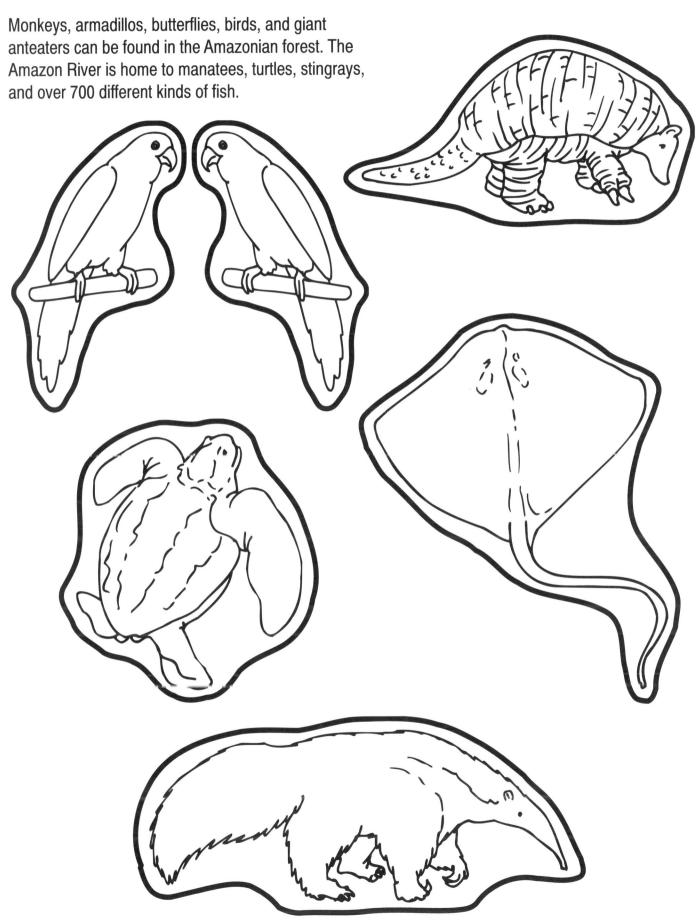

73

Bulletin Board Patterns: People of Brazil

Most of the people of Brazil are descendants of native Indians. Because the Portuguese were the first to settle in Brazil, Portuguese is spoken there.

Today people wear modern clothing in Brazil. However, on special occasions, such as holidays and festivals, people dress in traditional costumes.

Men known as *gauchos* (cowboys) wear baggy trousers, high leather boots, bandannas around their necks, wide hats, and wide leather belts.

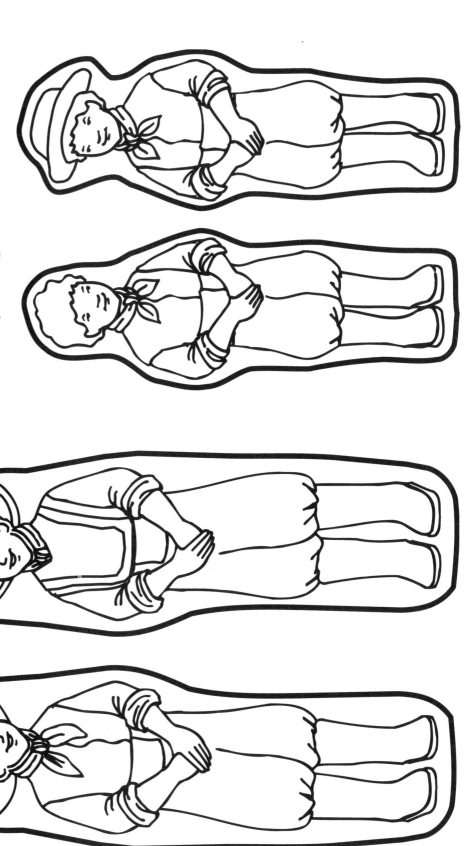

Bulletin Board Patterns: People of Brazil

Women wear flowing skirts with loosely fitting blouses. They also wear colorful headdresses and jewelry.

More Patterns for Brazil
Food and Transportation

Coffee is the main product of Brazil. Brazil produces more coffee than any other South American country. Corn is another important product of Brazil.

Transportation

Boats are used by families that live near inland waterways. Sailing ships are used to transport supplies.

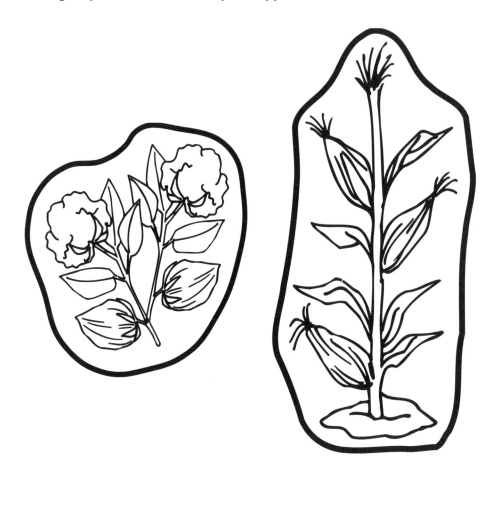

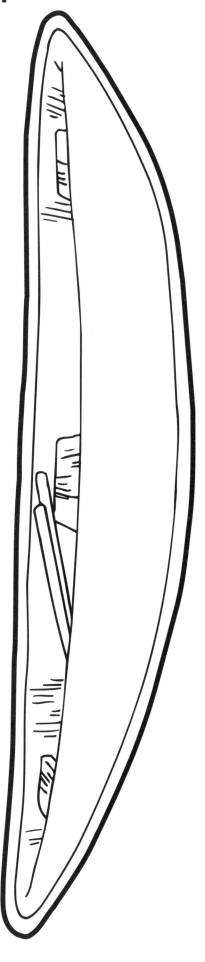

More Patterns for Brazil
Costumes and Crafts

1. **Ceramic tiles** are used to decorate houses and other public structures.
2. **Costumes** of bright and colorful designs are worn during the festival of Carnaval.

1.

2.

2.

More Patterns for Brazil
Festivals and Landmarks

Carnaval
The spring season brings the most important festival in Brazil, Carnaval. Special clothes, food, and decorations are prepared for this event.

Landmark
The capital city, Brasilia, is a landmark in itself. It contains many excellent examples of modern architecture designed by Oscar Neimeyer.

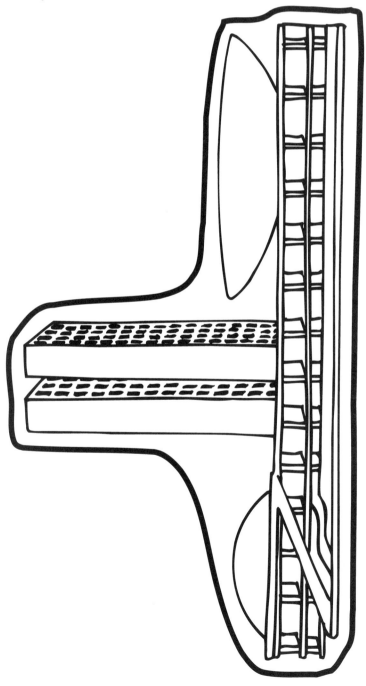

Brazilian Craft Activities

Let's Make a Brazilian Diorama

Ask each student to bring an empty shoe box to school. Provide paint and brushes for students to paint their boxes to resemble a place in Brazil.

Reproduce the patterns on pages 72-78 for students to color, cut out, and glue inside their dioramas.

When the dioramas are completed, display student projects on a table in front of your Brazilian community bulletin board.

Let's Make a Carnaval Headdress

Provide students with paper bags, paper towel rolls, paper plates, plastic containers, pie tins, and a variety of craft supplies such as sequins, buttons, macaroni, cloth scraps, pipe cleaners, markers, paint, and wrapping paper.

Share pictures of Carnaval and encourage children to design and create spectacular headdresses to wear or display in your classroom.

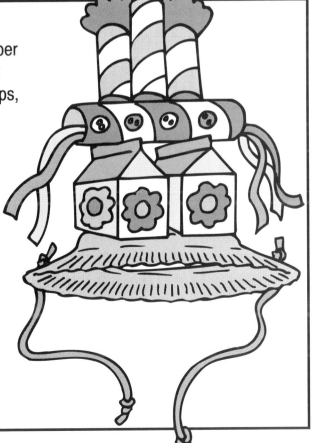

Brazilian Literature Links

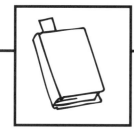

The Great Kapok Tree
by Lynne Cherry
Harcourt Brace Jovanovich, 1990

Brazilian rain forest animals try to talk a man with an ax out of cutting down their homes.

Story Hour Puppet Tree
Create a story hour puppet tree prop to introduce your students to rain forest animals of South America. Decorate a refrigerator box to look like a tree. Make brown construction paper pockets and attach them to the tree. Have students make a variety of rain forest animal puppets to fit in the construction paper pockets.

More Books About Brazil and South America

An Adventure in the Amazon
by the Cousteau Society, Simon & Schuster Books for Young Readers, 1992

Amazon Basin
by Jan Reynolds, Harcourt Brace Jovanovich, 1993

Amazon Boy
by Ted Lewin, Macmillan, 1993

Antonio's Rain Forest
by Anna Lewington, Carolrhoda Books, 1993

The Legend of El Dorado: A Latin American Tale
by Beatriz Vidal, Alfred A. Knopf, 1991

Moon Was Tired of Walking on Air
by Natalia Maree Belting, adapted by Nancy Van Laan, Houghton Mifflin, 1992

One Day in the Tropical Rain Forest
by Jean Craighead George, Crowell, 1990

South America
by D. V. Georges, Children's Book Press, 1986

This Place Is Wet
by Vicki Cobb, Walker & Co., 1989

When the Rivers Go Home
by Ted Lewin, Macmillan, 1992

Map: Modern China

China won its freedom from the Mongols in the late 1300s
and returned to its traditional Chinese culture. China's
freedom from foreign rule lasted almost three hundred years.
This period was called the Ming dynasty.

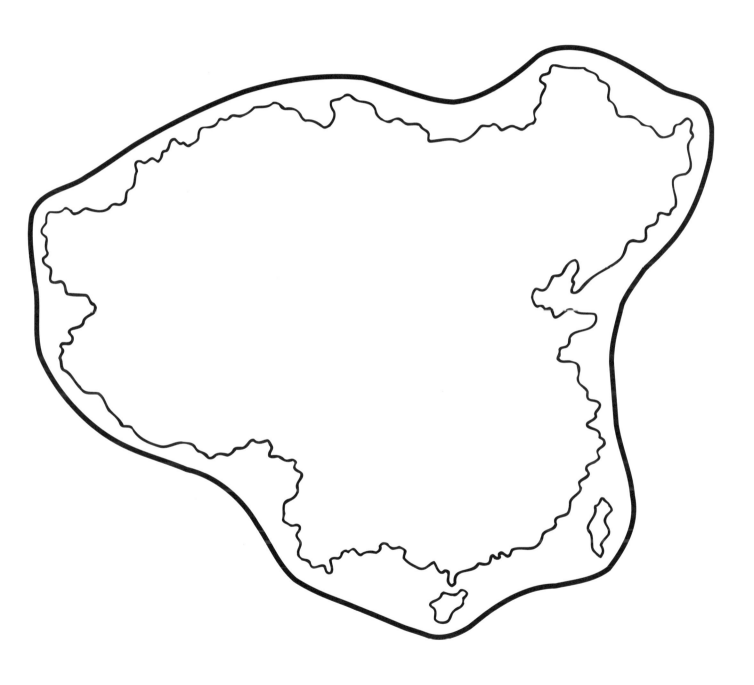

Map: Ancient China

During the Ming dynasty the capital of China was moved from Nanking to Peking. The Great Wall was rebuilt and the Emperor's Palace was constructed in the Forbidden City.

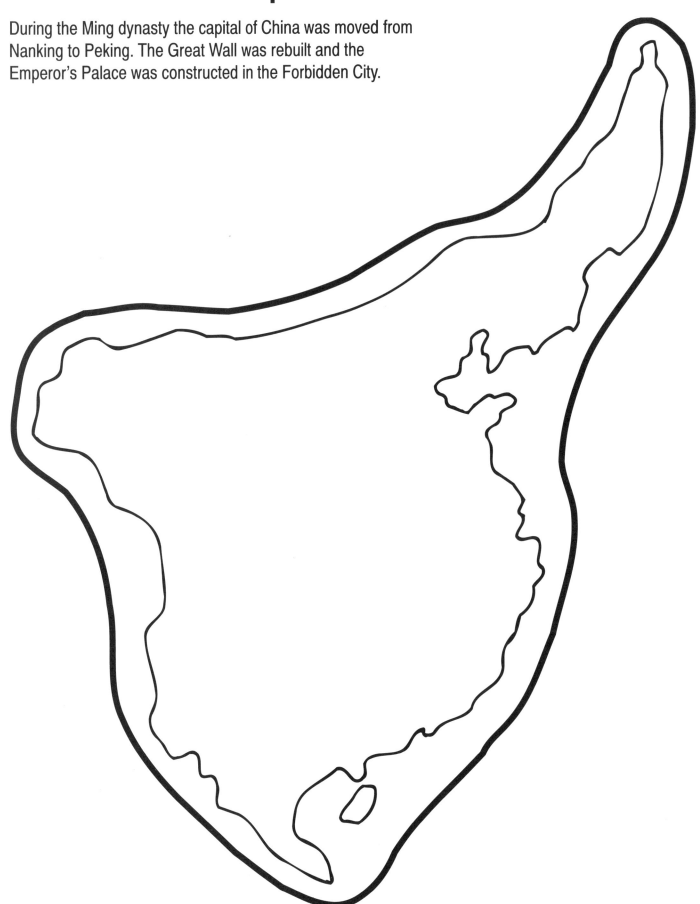

Bulletin Board: A Community in Ancient China

1. Enlarge the patterns on pages 84-90.
2. Color and cut out the patterns.
3. Cover your bulletin board with pale blue at the top of the board and green at the bottom.
4. Add a yellow or red colored border.
5. Enlarge, color, and cut out the title below.
6. Arrange and attach the patterns to your bulletin board.

An Ancient
Chinese
Community

Bulletin Board Patterns: A Dwelling in Ancient China

Homes in ancient China were simple one-room dwellings. These unique structures had swinging doors that were used as extra beds.

Bulletin Board Patterns: Animals of Ancient China

Animals found in ancient China include water buffalos, horses, geese, and fish. Many works of art created during this period include images of birds and fish.

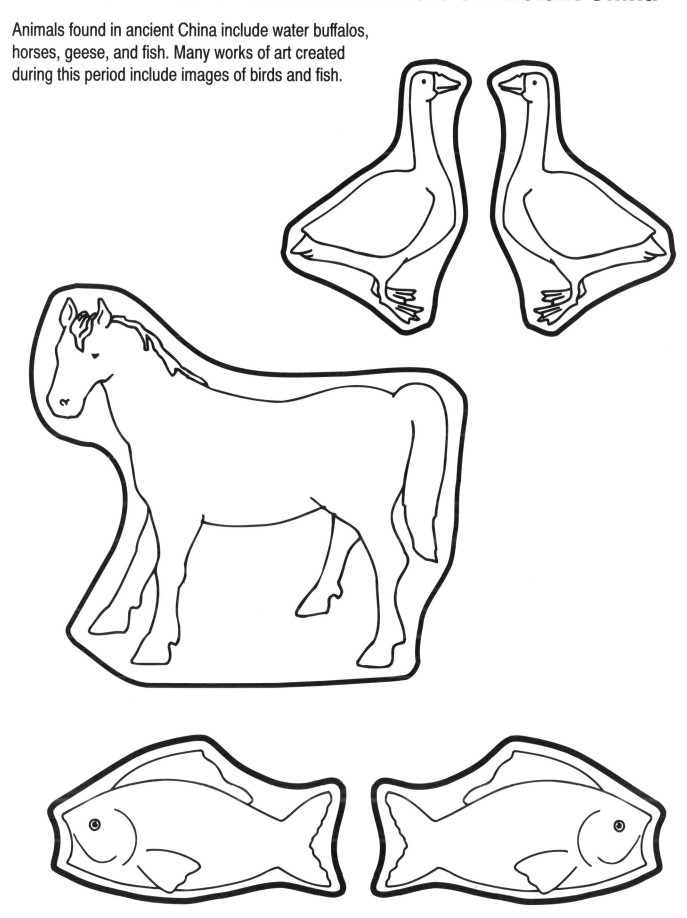

05

Bulletin Board Patterns: People of Ancient China

Wealthy people wore brightly colored clothing made from hand-woven silks. Commoners wore dark-colored cotton clothing.

Layers of clothing were worn by both men and women. As days grew warmer, fewer layers were worn.

Clothing articles included loose-fitting pants, a blouse or jacket, and a wide-brimmed hat. Sometimes long robes were worn.

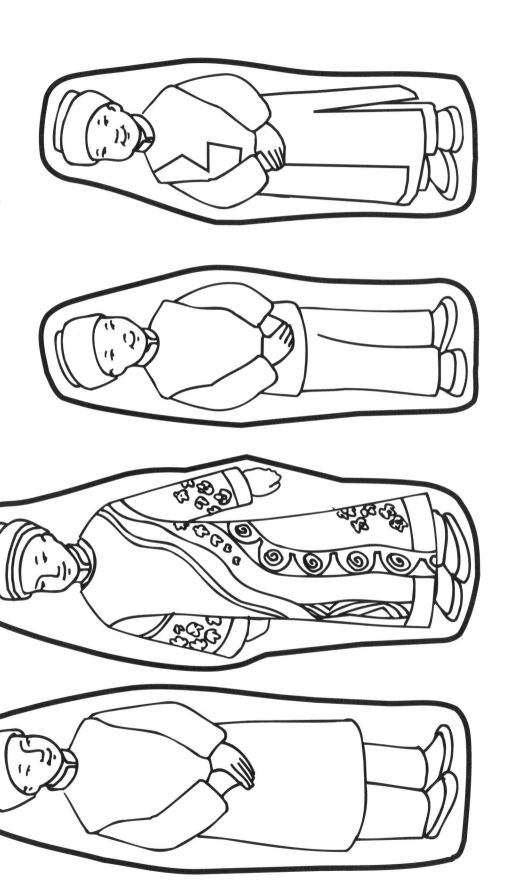

Bulletin Board Patterns: People of Ancient China

Because having small feet was considered a sign of beauty, wealthy women would have their feet bound at an early age to keep them from growing large. This made walking very difficult and often impossible.

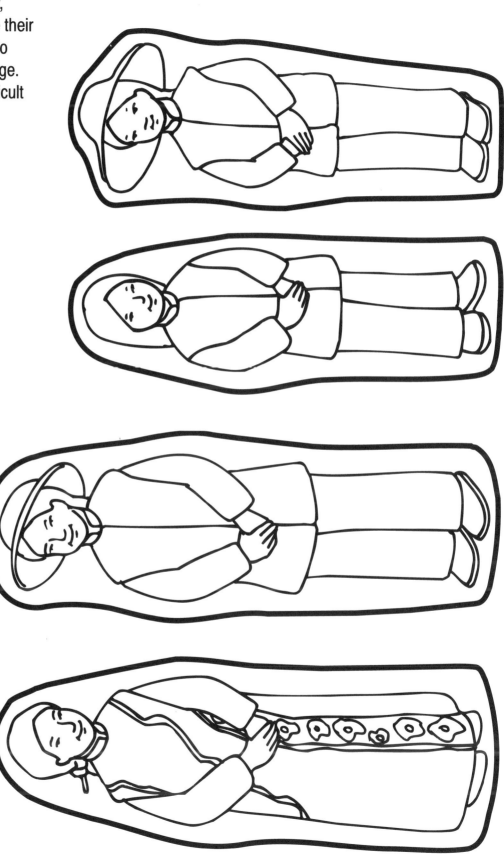

More Patterns for Ancient China
Food, Tools, and Recreation

Rice was an important product of ancient China. It was served boiled or quickly stir-fried as it is today.

1. **Lanterns** were used during festival celebrations such as New Year's Day.
2. **Pottery** was decorated with landscapes, birds, and other traditional designs.
3. **Kites** of all shapes and sizes were flown as a favorite pastime of the people in ancient China, especially during the Festival of Double Nine.

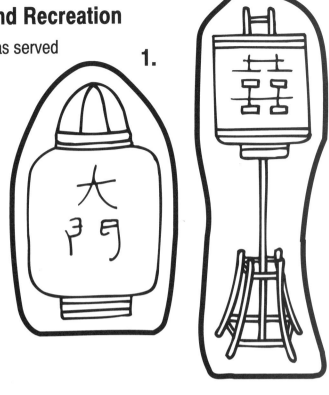

More Patterns for Ancient China
Clothing, Crafts, and Music

1. **Formal robes** were worn on special occasions.
2. **Jewelry** was made of jade and other gems.
3. **Musical instruments**, such as a variety of wind, string, and percussion instruments, were used during special ceremonies and festivals.

1.

3.

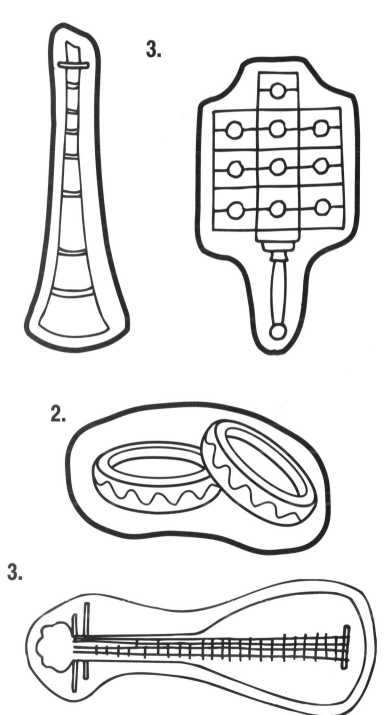

2.

3.

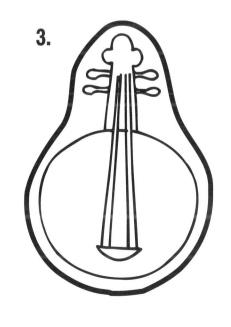

3.

More Patterns for Ancient China
Transportation and Landmarks

Rickshaw

Rickshaws are carriage-like vehicles that were pulled by runners and carried both people and materials.

Landmark

The Great Wall is called the Long Wall of Ten Thousand Li in China. This remarkable structure was designed to follow natural land formations and was built for protection against foreign invaders. The wall stretches 1,500 miles to the eastern coast of China.

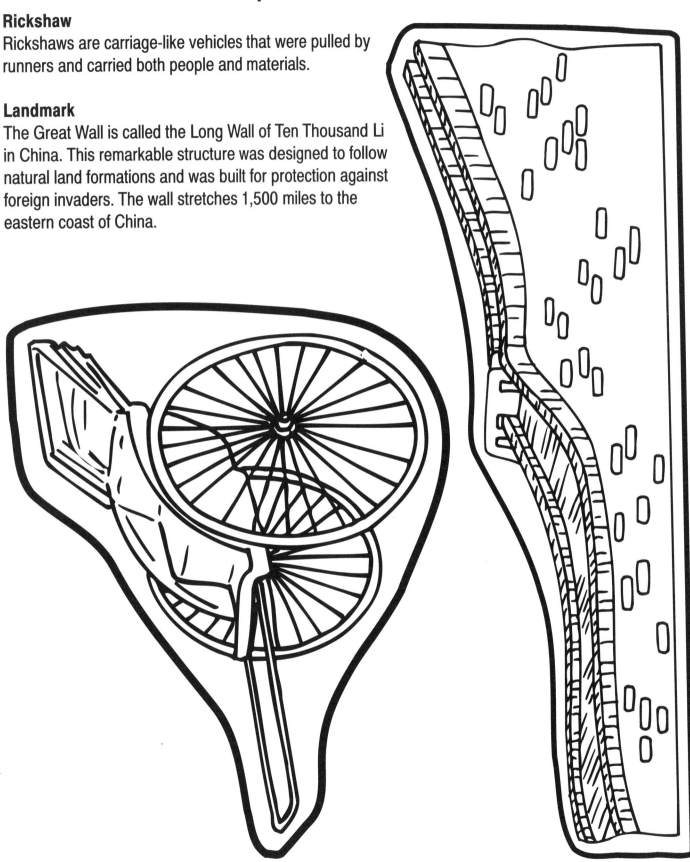

Ancient Chinese Craft Activities

Let's Make an Ancient Chinese Diorama

Ask each student to bring an empty shoe box to school. Provide paint and brushes for students to paint their boxes to resemble a place in ancient China.

Reproduce the patterns on pages 84-90 for students to color, cut out, and glue inside their dioramas.

When the dioramas are completed, display student projects on a table in front of your ancient Chinese community bulletin board.

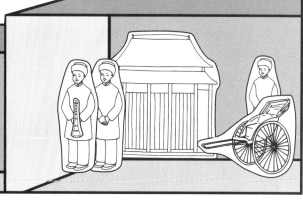
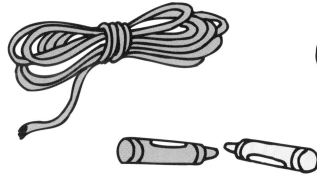

Let's Make Goldfish Kites

Enlarge the fish pattern on page 88 for students to trace on butcher paper.

Have each child decorate his or her fish, then punch two holes at the mouth of the fish. Provide yarn for students to lace and tie through each hole.

Hang finished kites from your classroom ceiling.

Ancient Chinese Literature Links

Why Rat Comes First
by Clara Yen
Children's Book Press, 1991

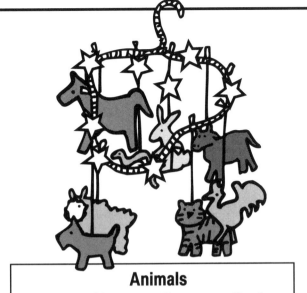

The rat thinks of a way to be first when the Jade King begins naming the twelve Chinese calendar years after his animal guests.

Chinese Calendar Mobile
Provide students with craft supplies and pictures of the animals listed to make Chinese calendar mobiles. Help students bend wire coat hangers into creatively shaped mobiles. Use yarn to cover the wire. Then glue stars around the mobile. Have children hang animals with yarn or ribbon.

Animals			
Dog	Sheep	Dragon	Snake
Horse	Boar	Monkey	Ox
Rooster	Tiger	Rabbit	Rat

More Books About China

China Homecoming
by Jean Frizt, Putnam, 1985

China's Bravest Girl
by Charlie Chin, Children's Book Press, 1993

Chinese New Year
by Tricia Brown, Henry Holt & Co., 1987

The Dragon's Robe
by Deborah Nourse Lattimore, Harper & Row, 1990

Everyone Knows What a Dragon Looks Like
by Jay Williams, Four Winds Press, 1976

The Eyes of the Dragon
by Margaret Leaf, Lothrop, Lee & Shepard, 1987

The Five Chinese Brothers
by Claire Huchet Bishop, Cowan McCann, 1938

The Great Wall of China
by Leonard Everett Fisher, Macmillan, 1986

The Jade Stone
by Caryn Yacowitz, Holiday House, 1992

Lion Dance: Ernie Wan's Chinese New Year
by Kate Waters, Scholastic, Inc., 1990

Lon Po Po
by Ed Young, Philomel Books, 1989

Ming Lo Moves the Mountain
by Arnold Lobel, Greenwillow Books, 1982

The Rainbow People
by Laurence Yep, Harper & Row, 1989

The Remarkable Journey of Prince Jen
by Lloyd Alexander, Dutton, 1991

The Seeing Stick
by Jane Yolen, Crowell, 1977

The Serpent's Children
by Laurence Yep, Harper & Row, 1984

The Story of Ping
by Marjorie Flack, Viking, 1933

The Year of the Panda
by Miriam Schlein, Crowell, 1990

Map: Modern Egypt

Egypt lies in the Middle East, in the northeastern corner of Africa.

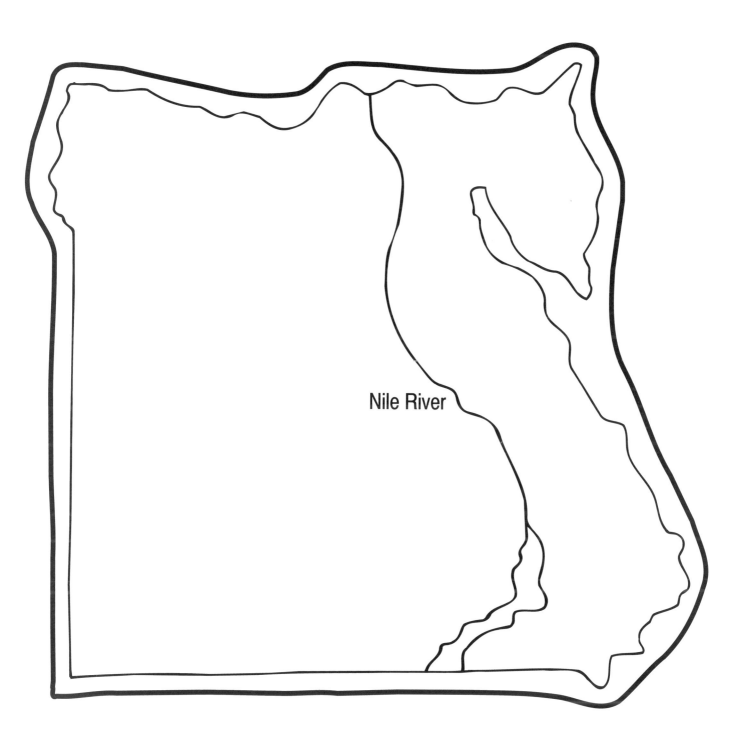

Nile River

Map: Ancient Egypt

Ancient Egypt occupied the Nile Valley. The empire reached as far south as ancient Ethiopia.

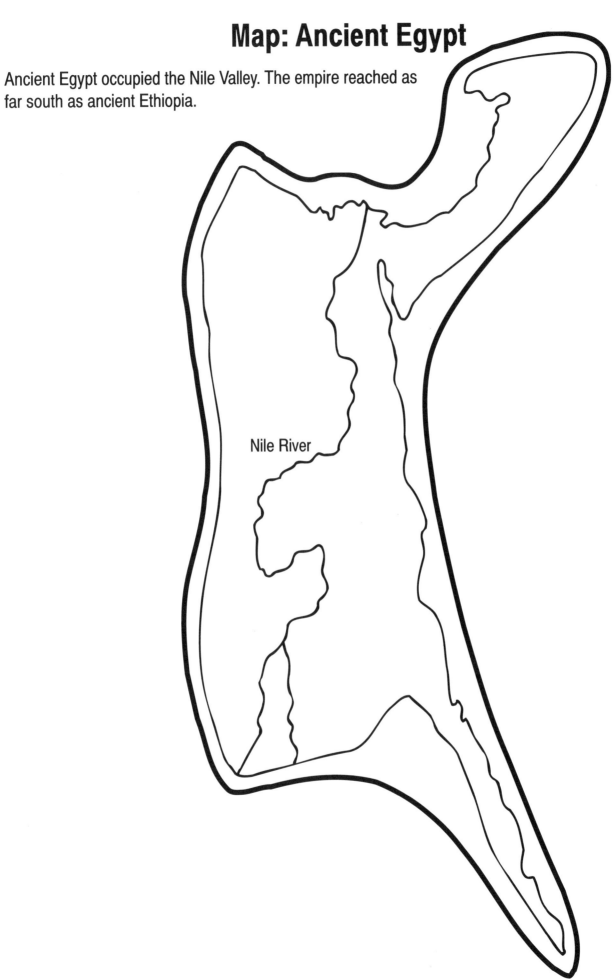

Nile River

Bulletin Board: A Community in Ancient Egypt

1. Enlarge the patterns on pages 96-102.
2. Color and cut out the patterns.
3. Cover your bulletin board with pale blue at the top of the board and brown or tan at the bottom.
4. Add a yellow or orange colored border.
5. Enlarge, color, and cut out the title below.
6. Arrange and attach the patterns to your bulletin board.

Bulletin Board Patterns: A Dwelling in Ancient Egypt

Ancient Egyptian dwellings were built of fragile, sun-dried mud bricks. When it rained, the bricks would crumble. The people would flatten the crumbled bricks and build new dwellings on top.

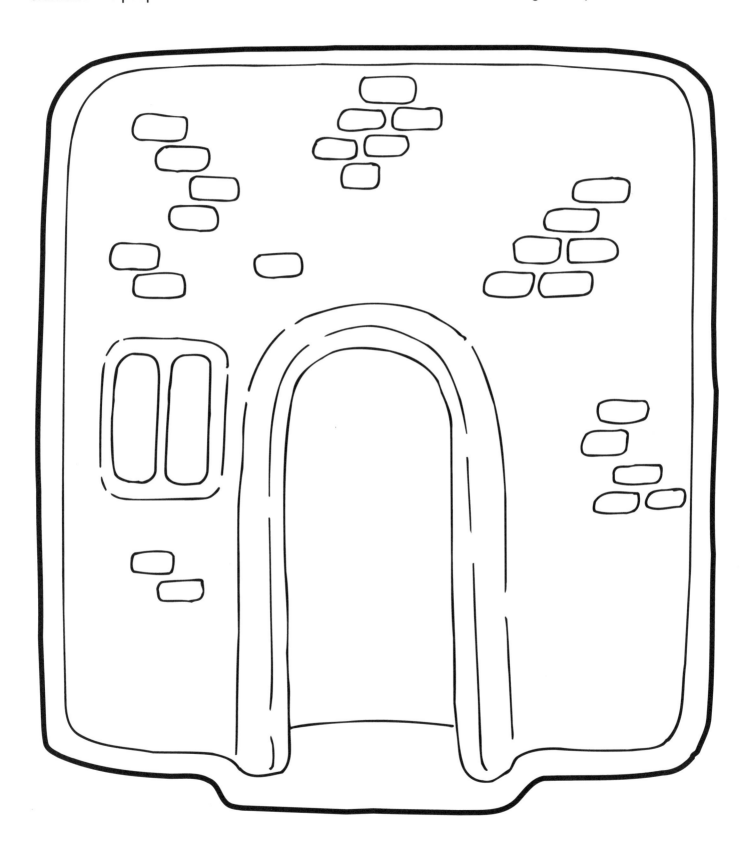

Bulletin Board Patterns: Animals of Ancient Egypt

The Nile region was home to a variety of wildlife including crocodiles and hippopotami. Ducks and geese were also found on the Nile.

Cats were important to the ancient Egyptians. They were kept as pets, and were trained to retrieve birds and control mice populations.

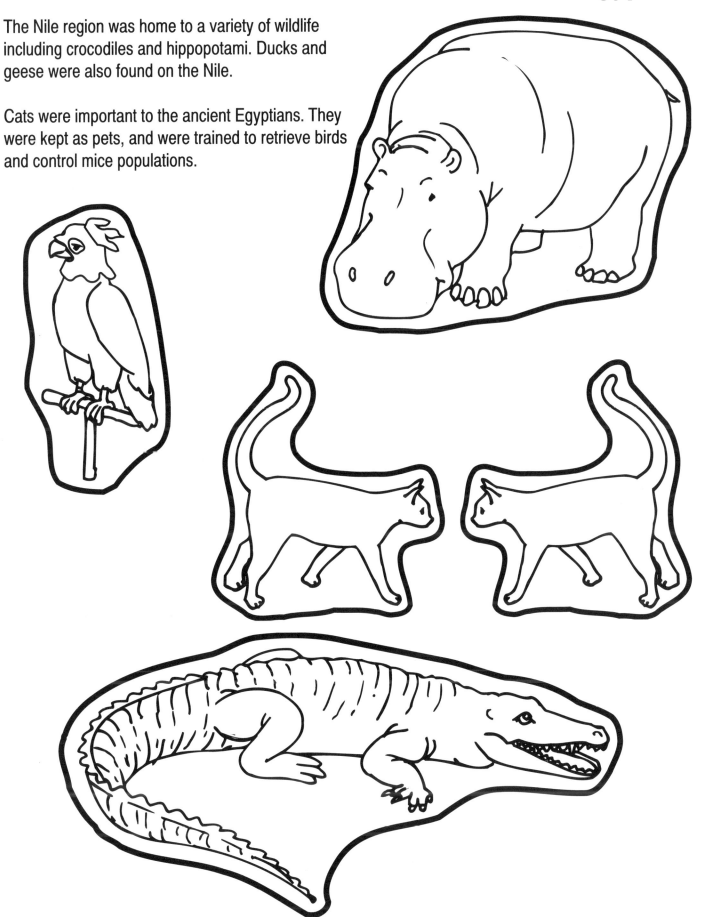

Bulletin Board Patterns: People of Ancient Egypt

Both men and women wore necklaces, rings, bracelets, and anklets.

Men wore a length of cloth wrapped around their waists.

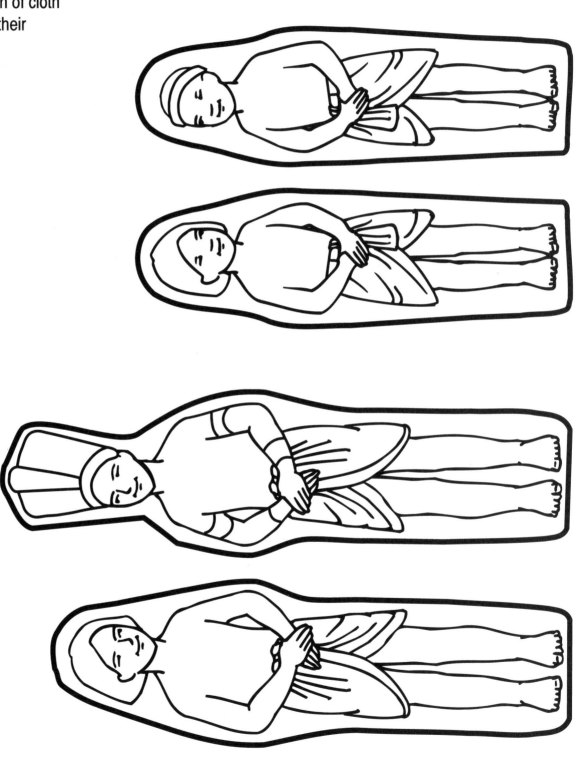

Bulletin Board Patterns: People of Ancient Egypt

Women made most of the clothing from hand-woven flax. Clothing was usually white or the natural color of flax.

Women wore tight, straight dresses with shoulder straps.

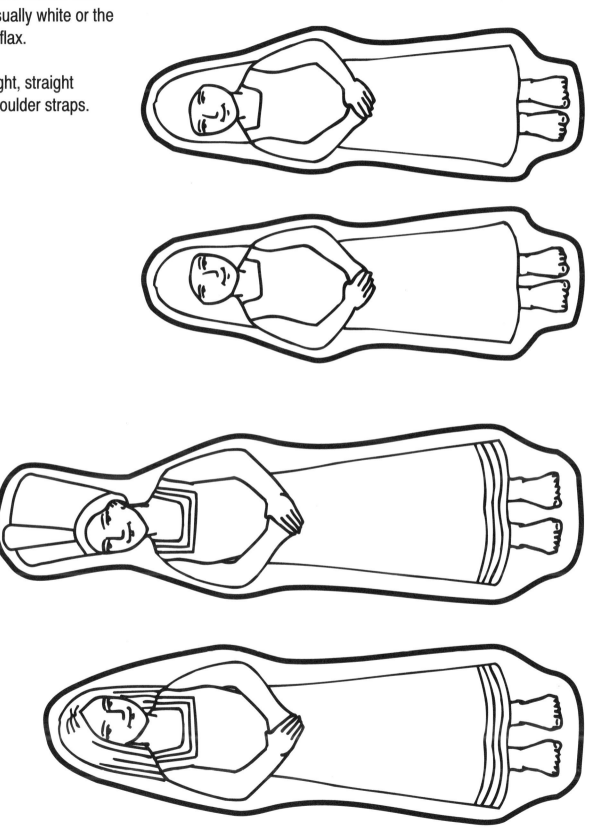

More Patterns for Ancient Egypt
Food and Tools

Apples, grapes, figs, beans, and grains were grown by the farmers. Bread was an important food to all Egyptians. Breads were mixed with eggs, nuts, and spices, and sometimes eaten with honey.

1. **Flint knives** were used to prepare foods.
2. **Baskets** were made from reeds and grass.
3. **Farming tools,** including plows, sickles, and digging sticks, were made of wood.

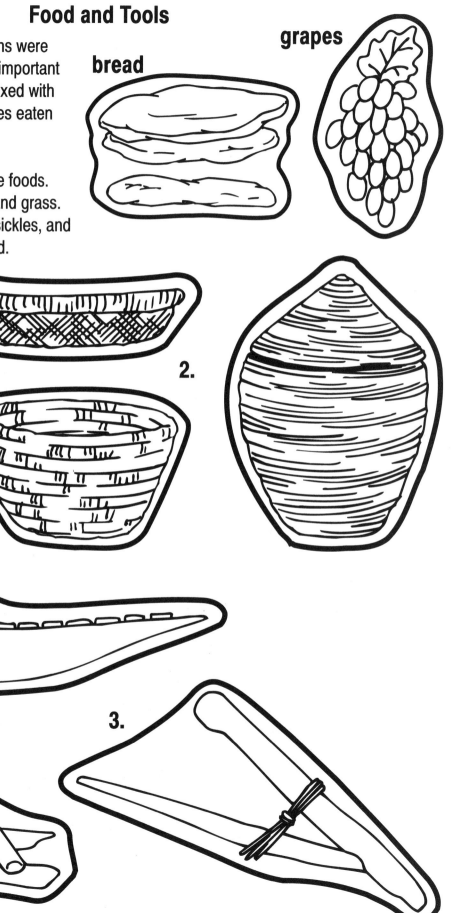

bread

grapes

1.

2.

3.

3.

3.

More Patterns for Ancient Egypt
Crafts and Symbols

Potters, carpenters, goldsmiths, and artists were all well-respected craftsmen. Many works of art were decorated with hieroglyphics (picture words) and images of animals.

1. **Jewelry** made of gold was worn by the pharaoh, or king. Common people wore jewelry made from other materials.
2. **Clay pottery** was used to cook, serve, and store foods and liquids.
3. **Books** were made using papyrus paper. Stories were written with hieroglyphics, pictures used in place of words.
4. **Sculptures** were often made of bronze. These statues were usually of wealthy people or of the pharaoh. Sculptures made of wood were whitewashed, then color was added.

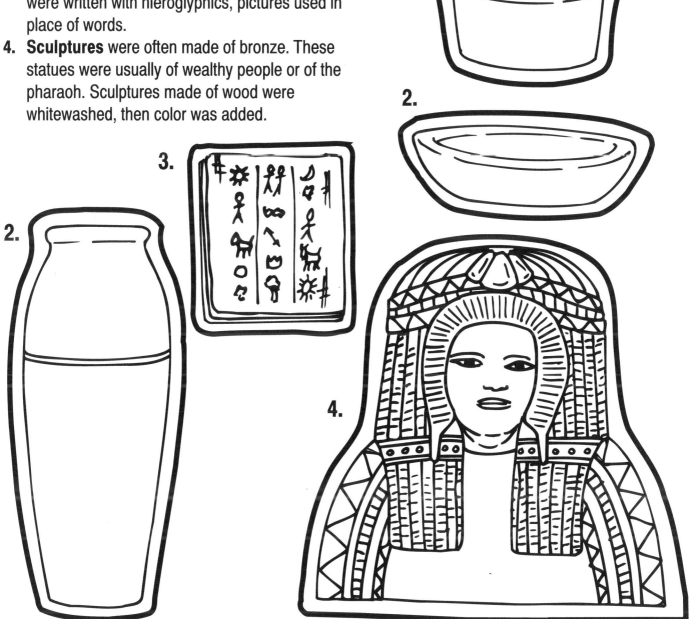

More Patterns for Ancient Egypt
Music, Transportation, and Landmarks

Musical instruments included harps, drums, and cymbals.

Transportation
Donkeys carried heavy loads on land. Wealthy people were carried in sedan chairs. Sailing and galley ships were used for water transportation.

Landmark
The Pyramid of Cheops, known as the Great Pyramid, is the largest of three ancient Egyptian structures found in Giza. This giant man-made structure was built as the resting place for the pharaoh Khufu. It contains over two million blocks that each measure about three feet square.

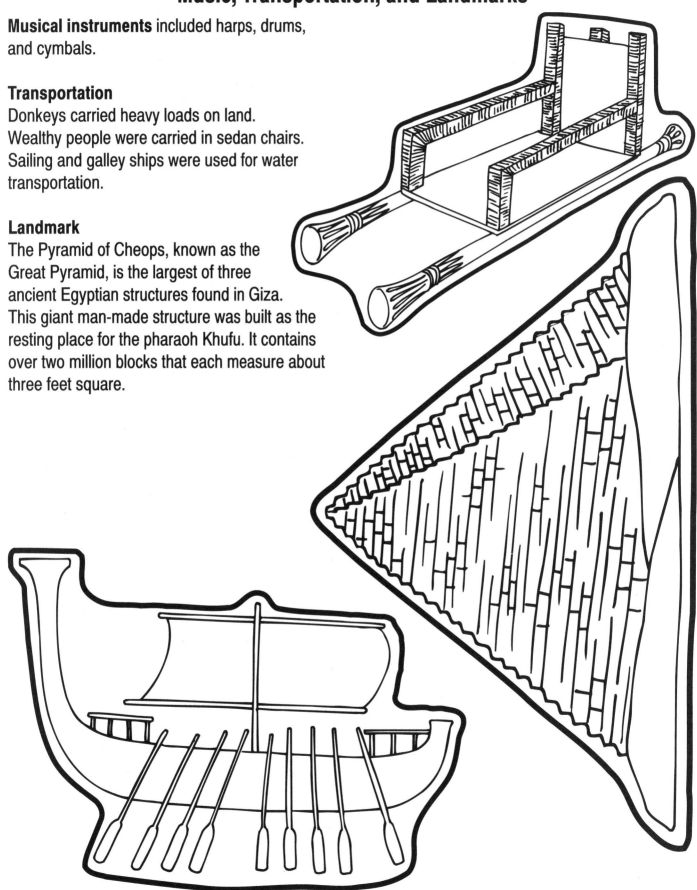

Ancient Egyptian Craft Activities

Let's Make an Ancient Egyptian Diorama

Ask each student to bring an empty shoe box to school. Provide paint and brushes for students to paint their boxes to resemble a place in Egypt.

Reproduce the patterns on pages 96-102 for students to color, cut out, and glue inside their dioramas.

When the dioramas are completed, display student projects on a table in front of your ancient Egyptian community bulletin board.

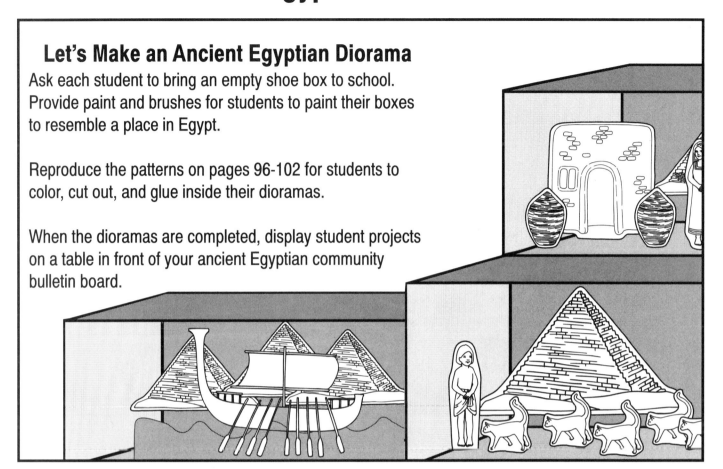

Let's Make an Ancient Egyptian Jeweled Collar

Provide students with large paper plates, colorful plastic straws, glue, markers, and scissors.

Show how to slit and cut out the center of a paper plate to form a collar. Then show students how to color the collar and arrange and glue on 1" plastic straw lengths.

Display finished collars on a bulletin board entitled "Jewels of the Nile."

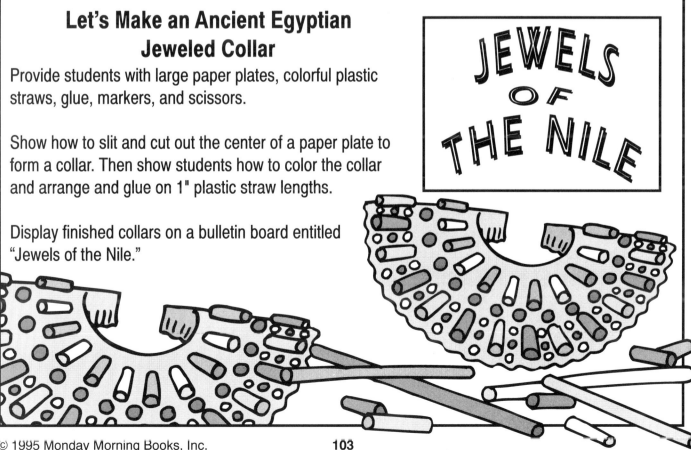

Ancient Egyptian Literature Links

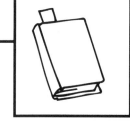

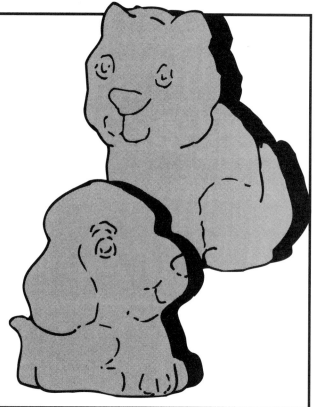

Zekmet, the Stonecarver
by Mary Slattery Stolz
Harcourt Brace Jovanovich, 1988

A stone carver works on a magnificent monument for a boastful pharaoh.

Painted Clay Monuments
Provide students with clay to form large blocks for carving. Invite children to make carved monuments of favorite things or people. Provide plastic utensils, large buttons, and Popsicle sticks to use as carving tools. Allow sculptures to dry. Then provide students with paint and brushes to decorate their monuments.

More Books About Egypt

Ancient Egypt
by Daniel Cohen, Doubleday, 1989

Ancient Egypt
by George Hart, Alfred A. Knopf, 1990

Ancient Egypt
by Judith Crosher, Viking, 1993

Ancient Egyptians
by Fiona McDonald, Barron's Educational Series, 1992

Ancient Times
by Amanda O'Neill, Crescent Books, 1992

Bill and Pete Go Down the Nile
by Tomie de Paola, Putnam's, 1987

Egypt
by Wilbur Cross, Children's Press, 1952

Egypt in Pictures
by Stephen C. Feinstein, Lerner, 1988

Egyptian Tombs
by Dr. Jeanne Bendick, Watts, 1989

Exploring the Past
by George Hart, Harcourt Brace Jovanovich, 1989

Fun with Heiroglyphs
by C. Roehrig, Viking, 1990

How People Lived
by Dr. Anne Milliard, Dorling Kindersley, Inc., 1989

Into the Mummy's Tomb
by Nicholas Reeves with Nan Froman, Scholastic, 1992

The Riddle of the Rosetta Stone
by James Giblin, Crowell, 1990

We Live in Egypt
by Preben Sejer Kristensen and Fiona Cameron, Bookwright Press, 1987

Map: Italy

Italy was once the center of the ancient civilization known as the Roman Empire.

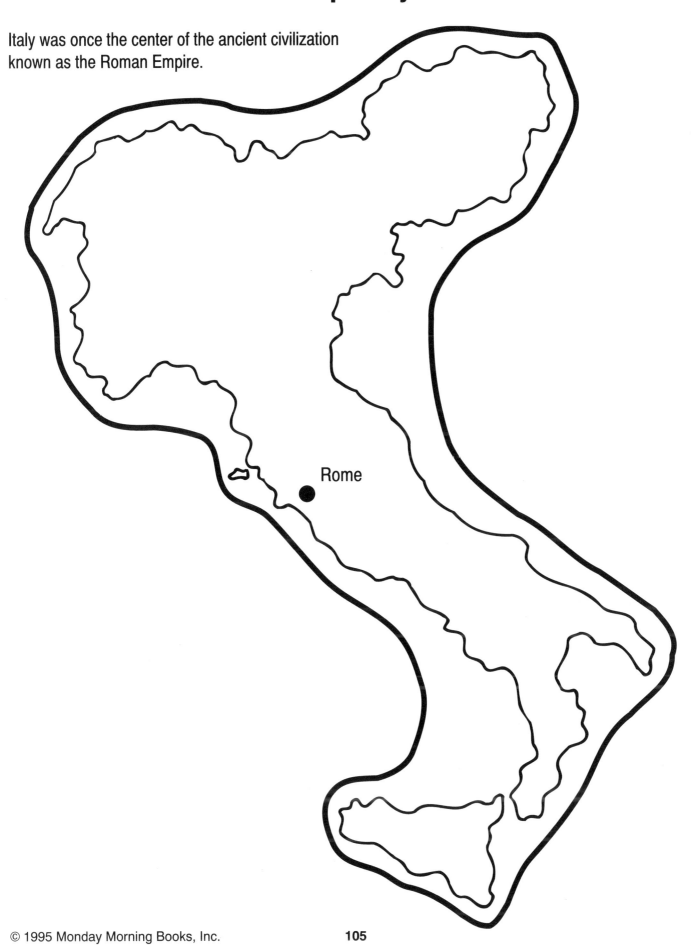

Rome

Map: Roman Empire

Ancient Rome is believed to have begun with a community of small wooden huts. The empire grew to include portions of Africa, Europe, and Asia.

Top

Bulletin Board: A Community in Ancient Rome

1. Enlarge the patterns on pages 108-114.
2. Color and cut out the patterns.
3. Cover your bulletin board with pale blue at the top of the board and brown or green at the bottom.
4. Add a yellow or blue colored border.
5. Enlarge, color, and cut out the title below.
6. Arrange and attach the patterns to your bulletin board.

Bulletin Board Patterns: A Dwelling in Ancient Rome

A home in ancient Rome was usually made of concrete covered with stone or brick. Most families lived in one-room structures called atriums. Wealthier families attached additional rooms around the basic structure making the atrium the center of the dwelling. Paintings called *frescos* covered entire walls in many Roman homes.

Bulletin Board Patterns: Animals of Ancient Rome

Animals found in ancient Rome include sheep, goats, oxen, donkeys, horses, and a variety of poultry (birds).

Oxen and donkeys were used to help farmers.

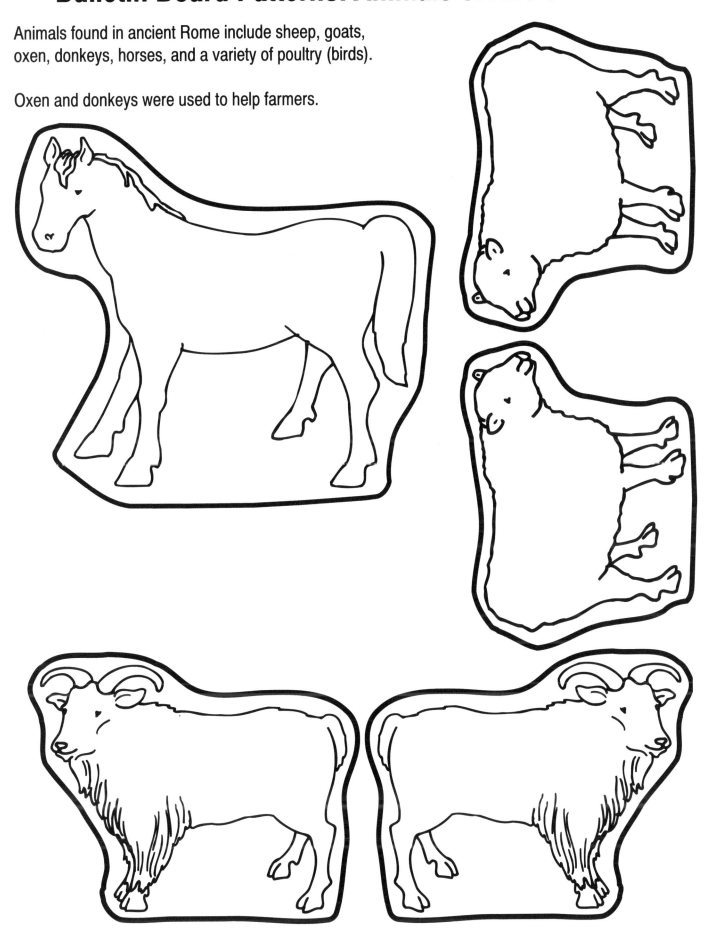

Bulletin Board Patterns: People of Ancient Rome

Romans wore draped clothing. Both men and women wore short, dress-like garments with short sleeves and sandals.

Men wore *togas*, oblong lengths of cloth worn draped over the shoulders.

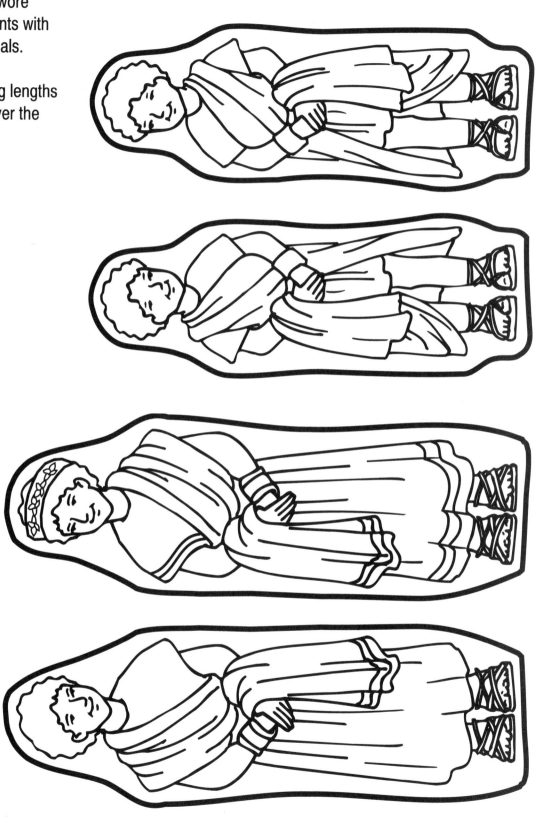

Bulletin Board Patterns: People of Ancient Rome

Roman women wore *stolas*, a tunic-style garment with clasps. They also wore fine jewelry made of gold, silver, and gemstones.

More Patterns for Ancient Rome
Food and Crafts

Wheat, barley, vegetables, and fruit were important products of ancient Rome. Olives and gold were other important products.

Bread was sold in shops that were open to the streets.

1. **Pottery** was used for carrying supplies and serving foods.
2. **Glassware** was used for storage and serving beverages.

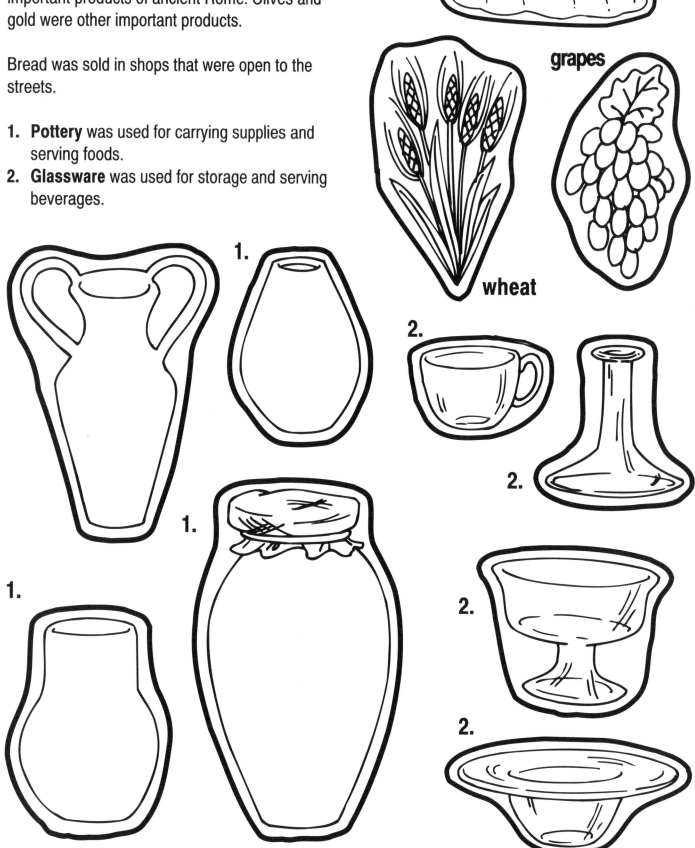

bread

grapes

wheat

1.

2.

2.

1.

1.

1.

2.

2.

2.

More Patterns for Ancient Rome
Clothing and Crafts

1. **Silver** was used to make a variety of products such as goblets, dinnerware, and helmets.
2. **Jewelry** was made of gold and silver.
3. **Sculptures** included realistic carved busts of people and carved pictures of historical events known as reliefs.
4. **Baskets** were used for serving and storage of foods as well as transportation of goods.

1.

1.

2.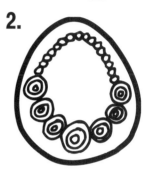

1.

3.

2.

4.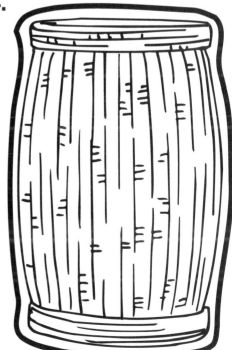

4.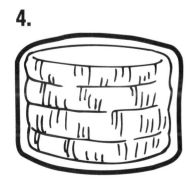

4.

More Patterns for Ancient Rome
Music, Transportation, and Landmarks

Musical instruments included flutes and a variety of stringed instruments.

Transportation

Wealthy people traveled in carriages. Chariots were horse-drawn recreational vehicles driven by gladiators.

Landmark

Ancient Romans were great architects. Although they did not invent the arch, they are believed to have been the first to use it successfully.

The Pantheon is an ancient Roman temple that is still standing in the center of Rome, Italy. This structure is an excellent example of how the Romans used the arch as an architectural element.

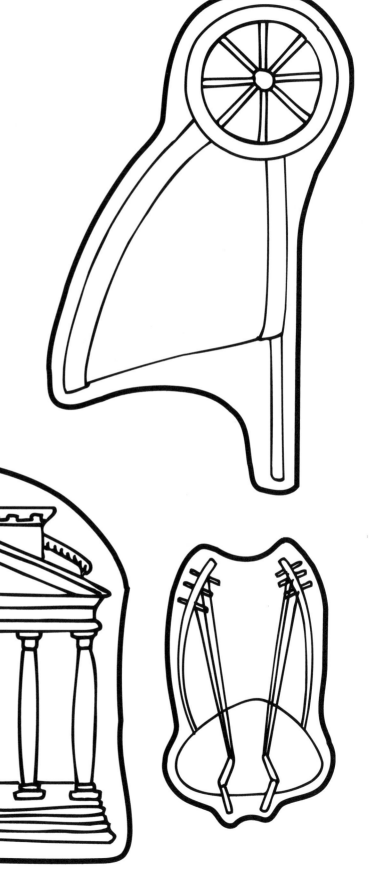

Ancient Roman Craft Activities

Let's Make an Ancient Roman Diorama

Ask each student to bring an empty shoe box to school. Provide paint and brushes for students to paint their boxes to resemble a place in Rome.

Reproduce the patterns on pages 108-114 for students to color, cut out, and glue inside their dioramas.

When the dioramas are completed, display student projects on a table in front of your ancient Roman community bulletin board.

Let's Make a Roman Fresco Display

Cover scraps of corrugated board with a thin coating of plaster. Provide each child with a plaster board, markers, paints, and a brush.

Share pictures of ancient Roman art with the class. Then encourage students to paint colorful scenes on their plaster boards.

Display finished frescos on a classroom wall and title the display "Frescos for a Roman Dwelling."

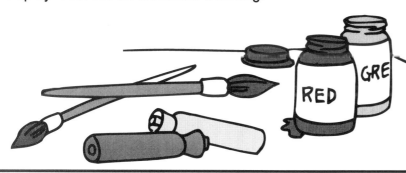

Ancient Roman Literature Links

The Talking Tree
by Robert Rayevsky
Putnam's, 1989

A king sets out to find a magical tree and instead finds a princess under a spell.

Imaginary Talking Puppets
Invite children to imagine talking to a tulip, an apple, a stuffed animal, or another inanimate object. Then provide craft materials to make hand or stick puppets. Children can use their puppets to share their imaginary conversation with the class. Encourage the class to ask questions during the presentations.

More Books About Ancient Rome and Italy

A Family in Italy
by Penny Hubley, Lerner, 1989

Ancient Rome
by Mike Corbishley, Facts on File, 1989

Ancient Rome
by Simon James, Alfred A. Knopf, 1990

Ancient Rome
by Simon James, Viking Penguin Books, 1992

Classical Rome
edited by John D. Clare, Harcourt Brace Jovanovich, 1992

Heroes, Gods & Emperors from Roman Mythology
by Kerry Usher, Schocken, 1984

The Legend of Old Befana
by Tomie de Paola, Harcourt Brace Jovanovich, 1980

The Mysterious Giant of Barletta
by Tomie de Paola, Harcourt Brace Jovanovich, 1984

Pompeii: Nightmare at Midday
by Kathryn Long Humphrey, Watts, 1990

Roman Forts
by Margaret Mulvihill, Gloucester Press, 1990

The Story of Befana
by Ilse Plume, Godine, 1981

Strega Nona Meets Her Match
by Tomie de Paola, Putnam's, 1993

The Talking Tree
by Inna Rayevsky, Putnam's, 1989

The Wreck of the Isis
by Robert D. Ballard with Rick Archbold, Scholastic, 1990

Map: Ancient Mexico

In ancient times the Mayan Indians lived in parts of areas known today as Mexico, Guatemala, and British Honduras.

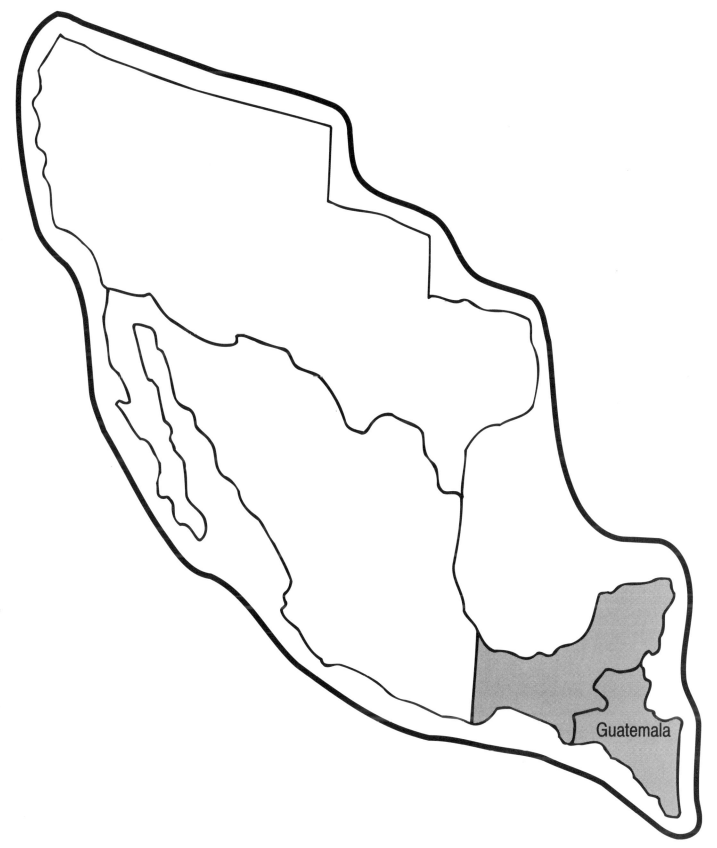

Map: Mayan Territory

The Mayans were the only natives of the
Americas to develop a form of writing.

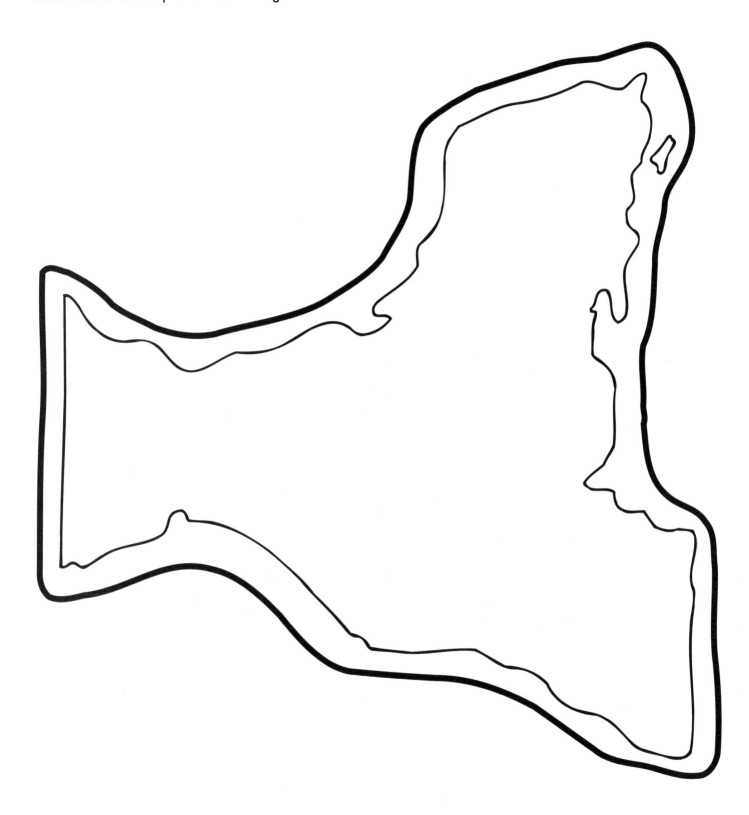

Bulletin Board: A Community in Mayan Territory

1. Enlarge the patterns on pages 120-126.
2. Color and cut out the patterns.
3. Cover your bulletin board with yellow at the top of the board and tan at the bottom.
4. Add an orange or red colored border.
5. Enlarge, color, and cut out the title below.
6. Arrange and attach the patterns to your bulletin board.

An Ancient
Mayan
Community

Bulletin Board Patterns: A Mayan Dwelling

Mayan families lived in single-room dwellings made from wood and palm leaves. These dwellings had no windows, and the roofs were thatched with palm leaves or grass.

Bulletin Board Patterns: Animals of a Mayan Community

Animals found in ancient Mexico include the quetzal, a bird found in the tropical forests, and domesticated turkeys and dogs.

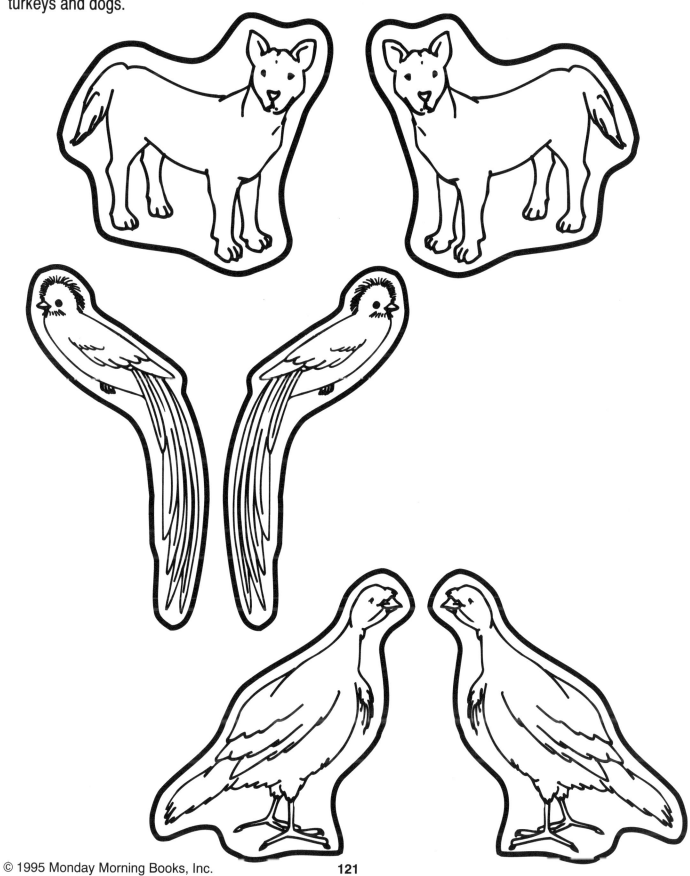

Bulletin Board Patterns: People of a Mayan Community

Mayan clothing was made of woven cotton. Garments were often decorated with paint or embroidery.

Mayan men wore loincloths with long ends in the front and back. During colder weather they wore blankets.

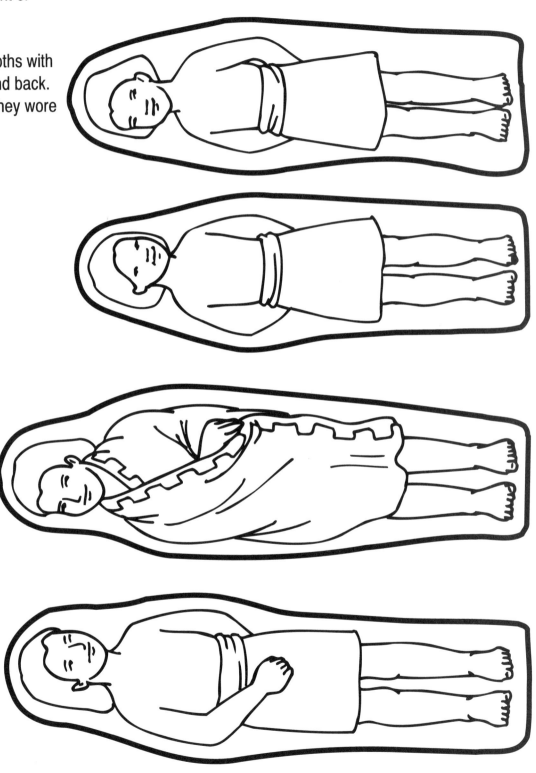

Bulletin Board Patterns: People of a Mayan Community

Mayan women wore skirts or
smock-like dresses.

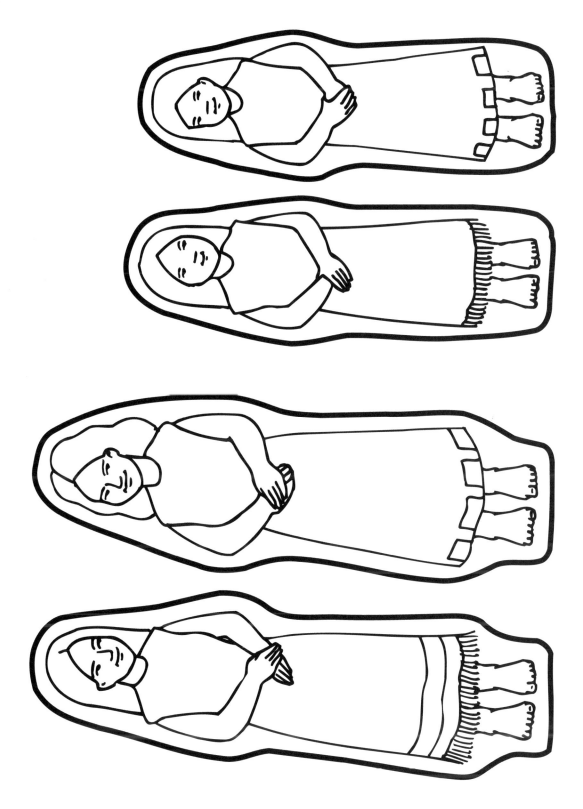

More Patterns for a Mayan Community
Food and Tools

Maize, or corn, was an important product in ancient Mexico. Even today, many Mexican foods are made or served with corn or ground corn.

Individual families kept hives of stingless bees for honey.

1. **Grinding stones and stone rolling pins** were used for grinding corn for meal.
2. **Baskets** were used for carrying supplies and serving foods.
3. **Stone axes** were used to cut down trees.

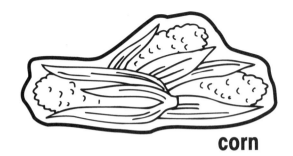

corn

1.

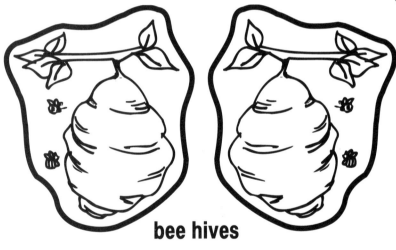

bee hives

2.

3.

More Patterns for a Mayan Community
Clothing, Crafts, and Symbols

1. **Headdresses** worn by Mayan leaders were decorated with colorful feathers from a quetzal.
2. **Jewelry** was made of seeds, shells, jade, and other materials.
3. **Clay pottery** was used for storage.
4. **Decorative pottery** displayed symbols or human figures. Pottery was used for serving and storage.

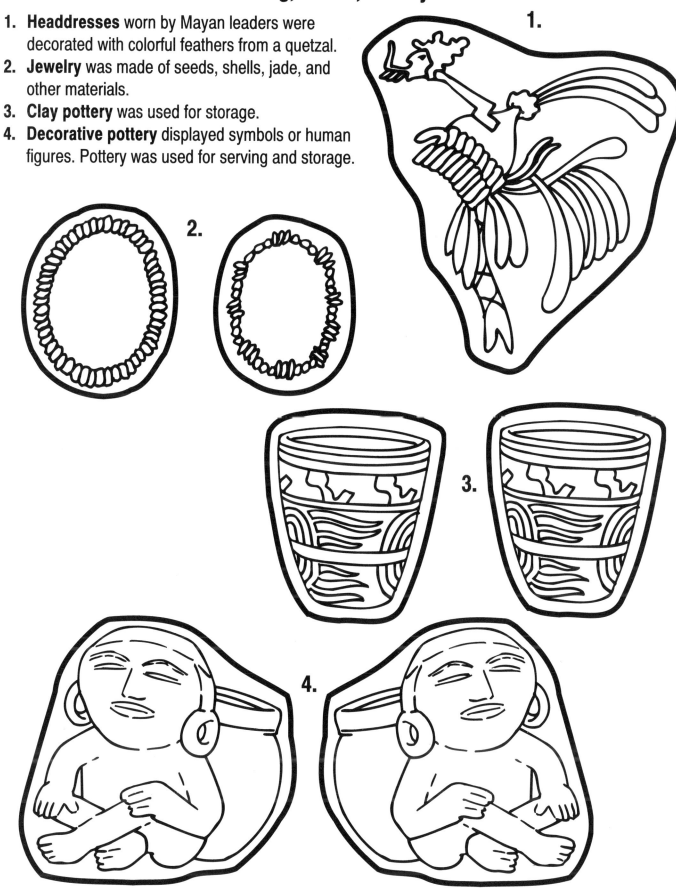

More Patterns for a Mayan Community
Landmarks

El Castillo, also known as The Temple of
Kukulcan, is one of the most famous buildings
at Chichén Itzá.

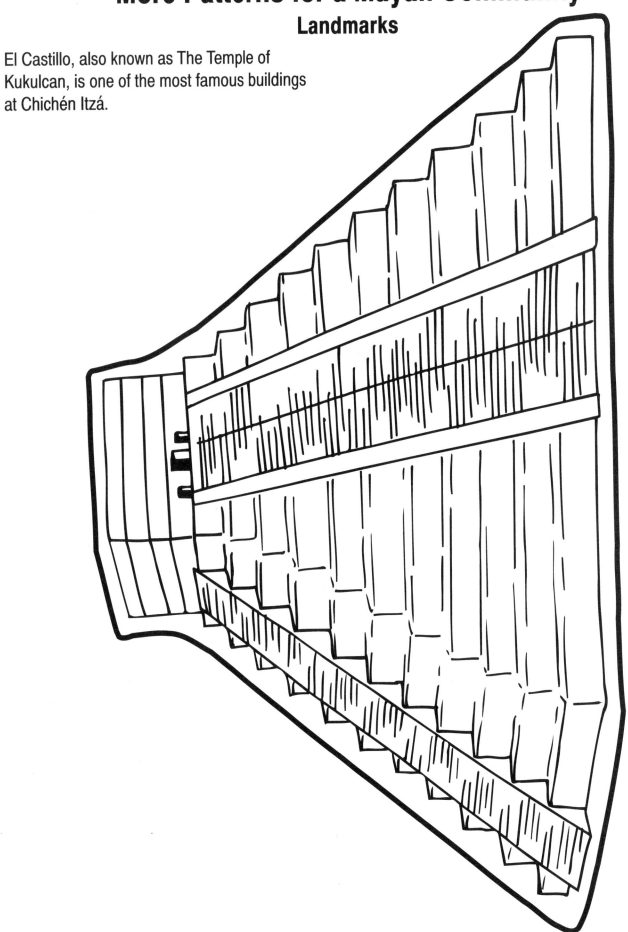

Mayan Craft Activities

Let's Make a Mayan Diorama

Ask each student to bring an empty shoe box to school. Provide paint and brushes for students to paint their boxes to resemble a Mayan community.

Reproduce the patterns on pages 120-126 for students to color, cut out, and glue inside their dioramas.

When the dioramas are completed, display student projects on a table in front of your Mayan community bulletin board.

Let's Make a Mayan Classroom Calendar

Cut a poster board circle and draw 4 concentric circles on the cutout. Draw a picture representing the current month in the circle.

Provide students with crayons or markers to draw pictures representing a day's events. Drawings could include weather, date, and activity icons. Encourage students to add as many details as they want.

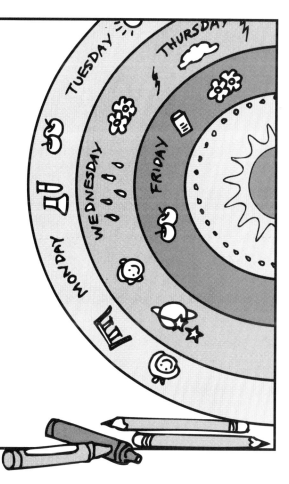

Mayan Literature Links

The Twenty-Five Mixtec
by Matthew Gollub
Tambourine Books, 1993

Residents of Oaxaca question why twenty-five cats move into their community.

Mixtec Cat Rewards
Provide students with folding cat patterns and craft supplies for decorating. Display cats on your bulletin board. Write a special privilege or activity on separate sheets of paper and place one inside each folding cat. When students are finished with assignments, allow them to choose a Mixtec Cat Reward.

More Books About the Maya and Mexico

A Family in Mexico
by Tom Moran, Lerner, 1987

The Ancient Aztecs
by Barbara L. Beck, Watts, 1983

The Ancient Incas
by Barbara L. Beck, Watts, 1983

The Ancient Maya
by B. L. Beck, Watts, 1983

Aztec, Inca, and Maya
by Elizabeth Baquedano, Alfred A. Knopf, 1993

Borreguita and the Coyote: a Tale from Ayulta, Mexico
by Verna Aardema, Alfred A. Knopf, 1991

The Captive
by Scott O'Dell, Houghton Mifflin, 1979

The Dwarf-Wizard of Uxmal
by Susan Hand Shetterly, Atheneum Books, 1990

The King's Fifth
by Scott O'Dell, Houghton Mifflin, 1966

Pablo Remembers
by George Ancona, Lothrop, Lee & Shepard, 1993

Pedro & the Padre: A Tale from Jalisco, Mexico
by Verna Aardema, Dial Books for Young Readers, 1991

Sky Watchers of Ages Past
by M. E. Weiss, Houghton Mifflin, 1984

Why There Is No Arguing in Heaven
by Deborah Nourse Lattimore, Harper & Row, 1989